Get Started in Drawing

Get Started in Drawing
Robin Capon

For UK order enquiries: please contact Bookpoint Ltd,
130 Milton Park, Abingdon, Oxon OX14 4SB.
Telephone: +44 (0) 1235 827720. *Fax:* +44 (0) 1235 400454.
Lines are open 09.00–17.00, Monday to Saturday, with a 24-hour
message answering service. Details about our titles and how to
order are available at www.teachyourself.com

For USA order enquiries: please contact McGraw-Hill
Customer Service, PO Box 545, Blacklick, OH 43004-0545, USA.
Telephone: 1-800-722-4726. *Fax:* 1-614-755-5645.

For Canada order enquiries: please contact McGraw-Hill
Ryerson Ltd, 300 Water St, Whitby, Ontario L1N 9B6, Canada.
Telephone: 905 430 5000. *Fax:* 905 430 5020.

Long renowned as the authoritative source for self-guided
learning – with more than 50 million copies sold worldwide –
the **Teach Yourself** series includes over 500 titles in the fields of
languages, crafts, hobbies, business, computing and education.

British Library Cataloguing in Publication Data: a catalogue record
for this title is available from the British Library.

Library of Congress Catalog Card Number: on file.

First published in UK 2009 by Hodder Education, part of
Hachette Livre UK, 338 Euston Road, London, NW1 3BH.

First published in US 2009 by The McGraw-Hill Companies, Inc.

This edition published 2010.

The teach yourself name is a registered trade mark of Hodder
Headline.

Typeset by MPS Limited, a Macmillan Company.

Printed in Great Britain for Hodder Education, an Hachette UK
Company, 338 Euston Road, London NW1 3BH, by CPI Cox &
Wyman, Reading, Berkshire RG1 8EX.

The publisher has used its best endeavours to ensure that the URLs
for external websites referred to in this book are correct and active
at the time of going to press. However, the publisher and the
author have no responsibility for the websites and can make no
guarantee that a site will remain live or that the content will remain
relevant, decent or appropriate.

Hachette UK's policy is to use papers that are natural, renewable
and recyclable products and made from wood grown in sustainable
forests. The logging and manufacturing processes are expected to
conform to the environmental regulations of the country of origin.

Impression number   10 9 8 7 6 5 4 3 2 1

Year   2014 2013 2012 2011 2010

Contents

Image credits

Front cover: © ULTRA.F/Digital Vision/Getty Images

Back cover: © Jakub Semeniuk/iStockphoto.com, © Royalty-Free/Corbis, © agencyby/iStockphoto.com, © Andy Cook/iStockphoto.com, © Christopher Ewing/iStockphoto.com, © zebicho – Fotolia.com, © Geoffrey Holman/iStockphoto.com, © Photodisc/Getty Images, © James C. Pruitt/iStockphoto.com, © Mohamed Saber – Fotolia.com

Meet the author

I have always been interested in drawing. Initially, in my youth, I made drawings simply for my own enjoyment, while later, as an art student, teacher, artist and now for many years as an art journalist, I have also recognized that, in addition to its potential as an art form in its own right, drawing is tremendously important as the skill that underpins all forms of art and craft activity.

You may be a complete beginner, or perhaps you already enjoy drawing but want to improve your skills to help you achieve even greater satisfaction and pleasure from your sketches and drawings? Certainly drawing is a wonderful means of expressing your thoughts and feelings about things. Or perhaps your main interest is painting, but you are aware that your basic drawing skills are letting you down?

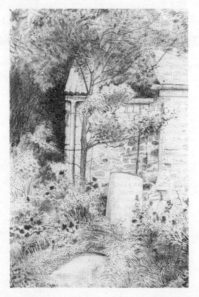

Illustration 0.1 There can be many different reasons for making a drawing. The inspiration is not always the subject matter itself but perhaps, as here, the interplay of different textures and light and dark effects. Charcoal and charcoal pencil.

Whatever your reasons for wanting to improve your drawing technique and gain confidence, I hope that this book will help. It considers every aspect of the drawing process, from the use of different materials and methods to selecting subject matter, composition and developing your own style of drawing.

And this is the key point, I think: there is no 'right' way to draw. So, once you have mastered the basic techniques and information covered in this book, don't be afraid to let your own thoughts and preferences play their part, and above all, enjoy yourself!

Only got a minute?

We are all born with the ability to draw. Essentially, drawing is making marks on some kind of surface. The inspiration for those marks may come from our imagination, or perhaps instead from seeing something that looks exciting to draw. In either case the marks are created by a process that entails translating thoughts and feelings into lines and shapes, using a pencil or a similar type of drawing tool or medium. The best drawings show both skill and interpretation.

Because we can all draw, given some time, practice and perseverance, we can improve our basic ability and the way that we express our ideas through the versatile medium of drawing. It is never too late to start drawing or to develop more skills and experience. One of the many advantages of drawing is the variety of possible approaches and interpretations that it offers.

People draw for different reasons and in consequence attribute different degrees of importance to the act of drawing. This makes a good starting point for learning more about drawing, and it is where this book begins. With an appreciation of the scope of drawing you then have a context in which to start learning more about materials, from the versatile pencil to various colour media, and key techniques, such as drawing with lines and using guidelines to construct specific shapes. You will also discover that an important part of learning to draw is learning to see, understand and visually analyze things. Building on this foundation of information, skills and attitudes, you will be able to progress to the later sections of the book, in which you can study the more challenging aspects of composition, working through different stages and finding the interesting ideas that will help you develop your own style of drawing.

5 Only got five minutes?

Whatever your reason for wanting to draw there is no doubt that, as you gain experience and confidence, you will find it a very rewarding activity. Drawing is a wonderful way of recording events and subjects that interest you, and certainly initially, it requires very little in the way of materials and equipment. There are many techniques and exercises to help you, but remember that there is no such thing as a 'right' way to draw. Successful drawings will owe as much to your individual interpretation as they will to your drawing skills and knowledge.

Pencils are a good medium to start with. They suit all types of drawing, from quick sketches to highly detailed tonal studies. Moreover, there are quite a few kinds of pencil to work with. In Chapter 2, there are exercises to help you test out your pencils to see what lines and effects are possible. Having gained confidence with pencils, experiment with other materials such as charcoal, wax and conté crayons, and pen and ink.

The next step is to examine ways of acquiring skills in basic drawing techniques, so that you can start using those materials with purpose and success, choosing the most suitable approach and effects for your subject matter.

The main techniques include drawing with lines. Contour drawings will help you draw with more assurance and pick out the essential shapes within the subject matter, while an understanding of methods involving guidelines will provide you with reliable ways of drawing cylindrical, symmetrical and similar basic shapes.

Another key skill is knowing how to make something look three-dimensional – creating a sense of form and space. First look hard at the subject matter and notice how the light plays on each surface and creates highlights and shadows of different intensities. Practise how to achieve different strengths of tone from your pencil, stick of charcoal, or other drawing medium, variations of pressure being the key factor. Use the exercises in Chapter 4 to help you develop confidence.

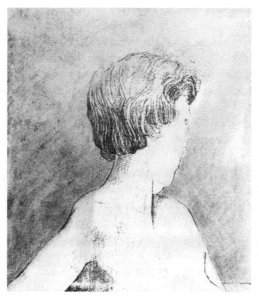

Illustration 0.2 Life drawing is a very good way to learn about the formal elements of drawing, such as proportion and creating a sense of three-dimensional form. Pen and ink with charcoal.

The principles and techniques covered so far equally apply to working with colour drawing media such as water-soluble coloured pencils, pastels and coloured inks. Again, it is a good idea to start with pencils, using a limited palette of colours to begin with and experimenting with ways of creating tone and texture effects. But do try as many different media as possible. It is mainly by experimenting that you will discover what best suits your approach to drawing.

Something that you will quickly appreciate about drawing is that you cannot draw any type of subject matter accurately if you have not first observed and studied it thoroughly. Always the starting point for a successful representational drawing is sound observation.

Linked with this is the practice of sketching. As explained in Chapter 7, a sketchbook is an essential item of equipment and, ideally, it is something that you should use every day. Sketching helps you develop your drawing skills and additionally you can use it for research, jotting down ideas, composition roughs and so on, working in different media.

There are two main points to remember about choosing things to draw: firstly, you are more likely to make a good drawing if the subject is something that you really want to draw; and secondly, always look for subjects that are in some way challenging, because this is how you will continue to improve your skills. There is only one guaranteed way to learn to draw and that is to have a go, and draw as often as you can!

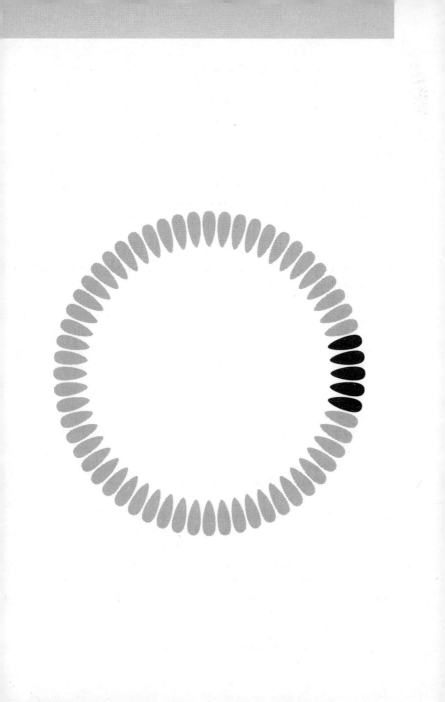

10 Only got ten minutes?

To an extent drawing is an innate ability: we are all born with some drawing skills and people have always wanted to draw, for it is a natural form of self-expression. So, in theory, we should all be able to draw! However, if you haven't drawn for a number of years, you are bound to have lost some skill and confidence. And even if you draw regularly, there are always fresh ideas to explore and new media to try out.

It is never too late to develop your interest in drawing and improve your technique.

Whatever your reasons for wanting to draw, it won't be long before you realize that there is an enormous range of tools, media and techniques to choose from. A knowledge of and confidence with these will provide you with tremendous scope for individuality and creativity.

The best way to learn to draw is to have a go for yourself, so throughout this book there are illustrations and exercises to help you. After studying the text, you may want to start by copying some of these examples as a way of practising and building up your confidence before tackling the exercises.

The first step towards developing your drawing skills is to gain some experience and confidence with a range of drawing tools and materials. It is best to concentrate on black and white media first. Pencils are a good starting point because they are a very familiar medium. See how many different types of marks and tones you can make with your pencil. There are many different types to try.

Next, try some drawings with charcoal, which is an excellent medium for creating a quick impression of a subject. And there are various types of crayons and inks which you should also consider.

From your initial experiments with tools and media you will be able to move on to gain some confidence and skill with the essential drawing techniques. The main techniques are line, tone, colour and texture. It is important to study these very carefully and to practise every one until you feel confident about it.

Line is the most commonly used drawing technique and the most versatile. Techniques include continuous line drawings and contour drawings. Additionally, lines can be applied in such a way that they convey a sense of tone (light and dark values) in a drawing, or, as guidelines, they will provide a sort of skeleton for the drawing – a starting point on which to build the accurate shapes.

For drawings in which you want to convey a good likeness of something, one of the main challenges is how to make things drawn on a flat piece of paper look three-dimensional. Working with contrasts of light and dark, and hence tonal values and shading techniques, is the main way of creating the illusion of space and depth.

Here, as always, the process starts with observation: note how the play of light on the subject creates different effects, from deep, dark shadows to glinting highlights. Make a tonal strip, as explained in Chapter 4, and then practise various shading techniques, such as hatching, blending, shading and erasing, and so on, before applying these to drawings of single objects, groups of objects and more complex subjects.

Tone is also related to colour, which is the next important topic to consider. The ability to use colour techniques will give you more scope to interpret the subject matter with the maximum impact.

The techniques so far discussed will equally apply to colour drawing media such as coloured pencils, soft pastels and pastel pencils. Experiment first, particularly with pressure, to get an idea of the range of light to dark and texture effects that are possible with each medium, and then try some sketches and drawings of different subjects.

Other interesting media include water-soluble coloured pencils, oil pastels, and coloured inks, which are available in both water-soluble and water-resistant types.

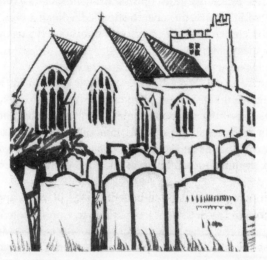

Illustration 0.3 As here, drawings do not have to be highly finished and detailed to be effective.
Ink brush drawing.

Having experimented with different media and practised the basic techniques, it is time to start applying what you have learned to making drawings of subjects that interest and inspire you. To begin with it is wise to work from actual rather than imagined subject matter. Observational skills are important for all artists because, whatever you want to draw and however you want to interpret it, you will make your most successful drawings if you start from a basis of knowledge and understanding of the subject matter.

From observation, you can progress to study related topics such as analysis, selection, interpretation and feeling, and adopting a more stylized, imaginative or even abstract approach. Even if you do not want to try these approaches just yet, it will be useful to appreciate the scope available.

To encourage you to draw regularly and to provide somewhere in which you can record ideas and information, you will need a sketchbook. This is the place for practising techniques, jotting down notes and ideas, and making sketches of interesting subjects at any time. Think of your sketchbook as your personal visual notebook. You don't have to show it to anyone else, and therefore you can work freely, without inhibition. Try to use your sketchbook every day.

As you begin to make larger and more complex drawings there are some aspects that assume a greater importance. These include design and preliminary planning. Theories of design and related topics – how to make composition sketches, for example, create an effective focal point, use a viewfinder, or work with a knowledge of perspective, proportion and related scale – are covered in Chapter 8.

Complex drawing projects often benefit from a planned approach working through key stages:

1 **Sketchbook ideas** – Rough plans and ideas to help with decisions about the subject matter and the sort of emphasis and impact you want to achieve in the drawing.
2 **Research** – Will you need more information to work from, in the form of reference sketches and studies? Which media and techniques will work best for the effects you envisage?
3 **Composition** – Try some composition roughs to examine a choice of designs before making your final decision.
4 **Preparation** – Will the paper need stretching or preparing in some way before you start drawing? Do you have all the equipment and materials you will need to complete the drawing?

When it comes to subject matter and choosing what to draw the scope is boundless. My advice is to attempt as many different types of subject as you can. And remember that you are more likely to make a good drawing if the subject interests you, rather than drawing just for the sake of drawing.

In time you will gradually begin to develop your own drawing style. This will be the result of a combination of factors – the media and techniques you use, your subject matter, and your own personality and how you see and react to things. As you begin to draw with increasing freedom and confidence, so your style will emerge.

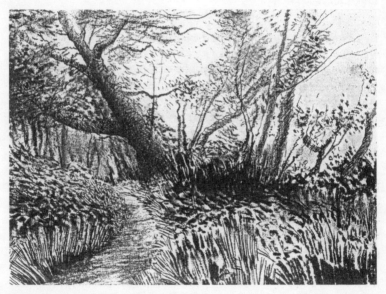

Illustration 0.4 Making a freely expressed drawing like this is a great way to convey your thoughts and feelings about a subject. Conté crayon.

You will soon discover that great sense of achievement and satisfaction when a drawing is completed and it exactly fulfils your expectations. What is more, a successful drawing will help to generate the enthusiasm and energy to tackle the next idea, which hopefully will be even better!

1

What is drawing?

In this chapter you will learn:
- *about the various types of drawings*
- *why drawing is important*
- *how drawings can express different ideas and communicate information.*

Making marks

Defining drawing is no easy task. But what we can say is that drawing involves making lines or marks on any suitable surface to convey ideas and information. Essentially, drawing is a means of expression and a method of contact between the artist and other people.

As you work through this book, you will notice that drawings can be made in many different ways and for a variety of reasons. Depending on the subject matter and what you want to say about it, you might, for example, choose to draw freely with a brush dipped in ink or instead work intricately with a sharp pencil. And, of course, you could decide to use colour or keep to black and white.

Sometimes a drawing is just a starting point, perhaps for an idea that you intend to develop later as a painting. Alternatively, there will be times when you want the drawing to make a fully resolved statement in its own right. Drawings can be informative, expressive or decorative, just as they can be humorous or serious, therapeutic or intellectual. There are cartoons and illustrations, plans and diagrams, roughs and sketches, details and studies. A drawing can be scratched in the sand or printed from a computer. There are many different media and techniques for making drawings; the scope is vast.

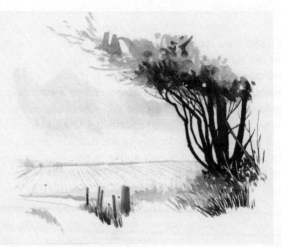

Illustration 1.1 The choice of medium is always an important consideration in a drawing. For speed, here I have chosen to work with a brush and diluted Indian ink.

LINE, TONE AND COLOUR

Contrary to the definition in many dictionaries, drawing is not confined to lines and monochrome. There are many colour drawing media and techniques to try, as discussed in Chapter 5. In addition, some drawing methods rely on washes or broad applications of tone rather than lines, and you can also make a drawing with a brush. In fact, often the initial stages of a painting rely on drawing with a brush, before any consideration can be given to colour, form and painterly qualities. Indeed, the boundaries between drawing and painting are never very precise.

In general terms, however, most drawings use line as the principle technique and they are made in black and white. The usual method is to press a soft substance, like pencil or charcoal, on to a harder, receptive surface, such as paper, to create a series of marks. As well, drawings can be made by an intaglio process, or by impressing, carving, indenting, spraying and other methods.

When we look at something we see it as form and colour, not in terms of lines. So in creating a drawing we have to assess what we see and then transcribe the image into a series of lines, dashes and dots. Although this process can reach heights of great sophistication, conveying likeness and realism, in practice all drawings must simplify, abstract and interpret what is actually seen.

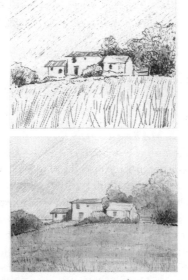

Illustration 1.2 These two drawings of the same subject show how the choice of medium influences the result. The top drawing, made with a fine fibre-tip pen, is free and expressive in character, whereas the pencil drawing is more controlled and offers more information.

Feeling and impact

What is a successful drawing? Perhaps, like many artists you measure a good drawing in terms of accuracy and realism, and you like the finished work to look as lifelike as possible? But shouldn't a drawing also express feeling and individuality? These qualities are important, I think. However, although we all have some drawing ability, it takes time to develop the necessary confidence to draw with real feeling and perception. The trouble is that as we grow up we tend to develop preconceptions and inhibitions that undermine our confidence to draw freely. To draw well, we need to overcome those inhibitions.

Most of us will envy the sheer joy and spontaneity that is found in the work of very young artists. There is nothing rubbed out, fussed over, cluttered or overworked here. The drawings of young children are characterized by clear and immediate statements about what is felt. They are acts of communication that are often easier and more successfully made than verbal expression. The marks are vital and telling. What a pity that we have to grow up!

Insight

Naturally, if you haven't done much drawing in the past, to begin with your drawings may not be as successful as you would like. But be assured, as long as you practise and persevere, success will follow.

MAKING YOUR MARKS COUNT

The more you draw, the more you will appreciate that successful drawings depend on doing just the right amount of work. A good drawing conveys the artist's message with some impact, yet at the same time will leave something to the imagination of the viewer. Simple drawings are often the most powerful. The best of these imply information that isn't actually drawn, combining this with lines of immense freedom and energy. Learning to simplify is a key element in the process of learning to draw.

But this isn't to say that every drawing must be reduced to a few lines. Often there are very good reasons to render detail, textures and highly accurate shapes. Why you choose to draw something and how you decide to interpret it are obviously important factors in determining the sort of drawing you make. It may well be that you have to use a variety of techniques and go into a fair amount of detail in order to express satisfactorily what you see as the essential characteristics of the subject matter. However, whether you use a few lines or many hundreds, everything should count and contribute towards the end result. Each mark should be vital.

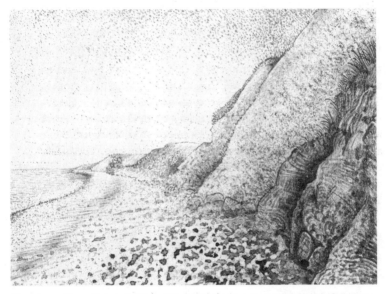

Illustration 1.3 There will always be plenty of ideas and techniques to try out in your drawings, so don't be afraid to experiment and to look for interesting ways to interpret each new subject. Pencil, wax resist with ink wash.

The language of drawing

There is a well-known saying that 'a picture is worth a thousand words', and how true this is! With most drawings, it would take many lengthy paragraphs to accurately describe their content and meaning. In contrast, we need only look at a drawing for a few seconds, and its message is conveyed almost immediately and most likely with more information and impact than any written description. What is more, the language of drawing is international – a drawing will mean something to us whatever our culture and background.

The fact that we can 'read' a drawing quite quickly need not lessen its lasting value. The best drawings never lose their appeal and, like any good work of art, there is always something that is interesting and stimulating to look at, and fresh qualities to understand and appreciate.

However, while there is a general language of drawing, there are obviously many subtle variations of that language from artist to artist. So, it follows that if we have an affinity towards particular artists or types of drawing it is because we respond more readily to certain ideas and ways of expressing them. Furthermore, each artist will usually employ variations of his or her drawing style according to the aims of the drawing. Working roughs are made to clarify ideas, sketchbook studies to collect information, and the final drawing to resolve thoughts into a visual statement. Each of these stages of working requires a different sort of approach and emphasis.

Types of drawing

Mostly we draw to inform or to express. For instance, if we want to show what something looks like, then we need to work in an objective and representational way. Alternatively, for subjects such as a stormy seascape or a dramatically lit interior, we may be tempted to draw in a much more personal way to express what we feel about the subject matter. This is classifying drawing into very broad types of course, for one general type does not necessarily preclude another. Drawings are often representational and informative, for example, yet not entirely objective, because they are drawn with some feeling. Similarly a subjective drawing, while perhaps very emotive in its impact, might equally convey pertinent information about the subject matter.

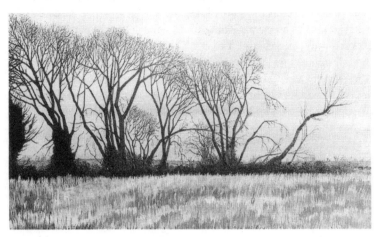

Illustration 1.4 Mood is a key quality to aim for, and again success will partly depend on the choice of media. Indian ink, charcoal, ink wash and white gouache.

Drawings that inform normally result from straightforward observation and enquiry. Such drawings aim to create records of fact, and this process is sometimes carried further into detailed analysis. In contrast, where the artist's personal response to the subject dominates, emotion is likely to replace an emphasis on observation and, as a result, the work becomes much more expressive and individual in nature, perhaps to the extent that the final drawing shows a completely non-objective or abstract quality.

Insight

While detailed, perhaps 'photographic' drawings can be admired for their technical skill, they are not always the most interesting and appealing to look at. Drawings are best when they reflect something of the individual artist.

MEDIUM AND METHOD

In response to the subject matter and our aims and objectives for undertaking the drawing, we have to decide which method is best suited to realize the idea fully. Vital to the success of any drawing is the medium we choose and the consequent range of techniques. So, as well as being objective or subjective, representational or expressive, analytical or stylized, decorative or abstract, drawings can also be classified by medium and method: pencil, pen and ink, charcoal, mixed media, and so on. There are also line drawings, tonal drawings, line and wash, and a range of other techniques. And, as previously mentioned, drawing types may be thumbnail sketches, diagrammatic summaries, roughs, cartoons, details, under-drawing for painting, research studies and large-scale completed works.

Insight

'Medium' is a term that has several meanings. Mostly, we think of medium as the material used to make the drawing, such as pencil or ink. But it can also mean the process itself, such as drawing or painting, or a substance that is added to paint to alter its character, such as glaze medium or retarding medium.

So, before you begin a drawing, it is wise to plan it in terms of:

- ▶ **approach** – *objective or subjective*
- ▶ **method** – *pencil, line and wash, etc.*
- ▶ **outcome** – *sketch, study, highly resolved drawing, etc.*

You will begin to understand more about the range of available materials and the different ways of looking and selecting when you have studied the next few chapters.

Master drawings

Throughout history artists have used whatever tools and techniques were available to express their observations, thoughts, emotions and anxieties in the form of drawings. Cave drawings have been found dating back to some 40,000 years ago. Many early drawings were decorative, being scratched on to pottery, walls or columns, for example, or engraved into metal or carved from wood. Few examples of drawings on paper or parchment exist before the sixteenth century.

The 'modern' age of drawing began with the invention of printing and the woodcut. Artists such as Dürer could reach a much wider audience through their illustrations in books and as separate reproductions. But it was during the Renaissance period of the fifteenth and sixteenth centuries that drawing was seen as an art form in its own right and as the basis for all art. Uccello, Leonardo da Vinci, Michelangelo, Raphael and Holbein were among many notable artists of that time who sought to perfect devices such as perspective, find means of achieving correct proportions, and explore techniques like silverpoint, chalk and charcoal drawing.

As in many other art forms, the history of drawing reflects the outlook and wealth of different ages. There are periods when portrait drawings were fashionable and others when artists were more concerned with nature, religion or the mysteries of the universe. There were times of reaction and invention as well as of celebration and consolidation. Obviously, the history of drawing is a very extensive subject, so if you come across well-known artists whose drawings you find interesting and inspiring then do a little detective work of your own. See what more you can find out about their life and work. Study their subjects and techniques; perhaps these will inform your own approach to drawing. Clearly, some artists will appeal to you more than others, so find time to borrow books from your local library and begin to develop an appreciation of different artists and styles.

Looking and learning

As well as being very enjoyable and rewarding, looking at a variety of drawings made by other artists will help inspire and influence your own work and teach you a great deal about selecting subjects, using techniques and presenting drawings to the best advantage.

Looking at drawings is a good habit to develop and it should play an important part in learning to draw. So try to view a wide range of work – drawings by your friends as well as those of the great masters. Visit exhibitions, galleries and museums. Go to local exhibitions as well as to see the collections at the British Museum, Courtauld Institute, Ashmolean and other major galleries. In fact, many provincial museums have a surprisingly large and interesting collection of drawings to view.

Try to keep an open mind about the various approaches to drawing, and therefore look at as many different types as possible. Study each drawing to see what you like or dislike about the composition, use of media, impact and so on, and whether it can provide any indicators for your own work. Looking at other artists' drawings helps us to form opinions and shape our own philosophy and outlook. Equally, it can be inspirational, can clarify a problem that we have been struggling with for some while, or perhaps suggest a fresh way forward.

RESEARCH

There are numerous famous artists whose drawings are worth studying. A comprehensive list of such artists would be extremely lengthy, although it could well include the following: Poussin, Claude Lorrain, Rubens, Rembrandt, Gainsborough, Goya, Daumier, Degas, Cézanne, Gauguin, Toulouse-Lautrec, Matisse, Picasso, Klee and Hockney.

As you look at the drawings by these and other artists, try to put your personal preferences aside for a moment: try to view each drawing on its individual merits. And while there are obvious benefits from studying such drawings, I should not want to give the impression that the benefits are exclusively to do with helping us develop our own drawing technique. Drawings are also for enjoyment, and remember, to fully appreciate a good drawing you may need to look at it many times.

Why do we draw?

From using flints on cave walls to making sophisticated images on computers, people have always felt the need to draw. It is a natural form of expression and communication. We draw out of curiosity and interest, to help us understand things, solve problems, record information or resolve ideas. Ideally, we draw because there is an urge, an inspiration, a desire to commit ideas to paper. It is a great way of showing what we think and feel about things.

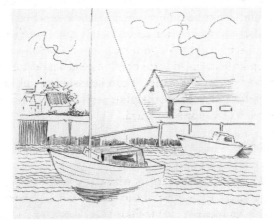

Illustration 1.5 One advantage of drawing is that it does not require a lot of complicated or expensive equipment. It can be a very immediate and straightforward process. Ball-point pen.

Drawing isn't always easy: it can be very demanding and difficult. But it should always be rewarding. Already you will have an indication of the exciting scope of drawing. Whatever philosophy you evolve towards the subject, you will find that there are plenty of ideas and techniques to choose from – there is something for everyone. And the more involved you become with drawing and the more you practise, the greater will be your enjoyment. You will soon discover that tremendous sense of achievement and satisfaction when a drawing is completed and it exactly states your intentions. What's more, a successful drawing will help to generate the enthusiasm and energy to tackle the next idea, which of course should be even better!

However, to draw well depends on a number of factors and qualities, not least of which is self-confidence. Drawings always seem to work best if they can be expressed freely and positively. Naturally, it will take you a little time to build up some confidence, which will develop mainly from your experiences of different media, techniques, and drawing subjects and situations. Here, the best advice I can give is to be patient and persevering. Obviously, in trying out various ideas and approaches you will make mistakes and there will be frustrations and disappointments to overcome before you can start to show real progress. But with application and determination you will quickly improve your drawing skills.

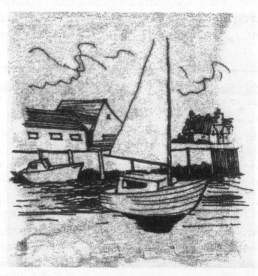

Illustration 1.6 Based on the same subject matter as Illustration 1.5, this is a monoprint drawing. It was made by gently lowering the paper over an area of printing ink rolled out on a sheet of glass. The drawing was made with a sharp pencil and then the paper was carefully removed to reveal the reversed and more interesting drawing on the back.

CHALLENGE AND MOTIVATION

The challenge of drawing is part of its attraction. If you try to make it easy by sticking to simple methods and familiar subjects then all you will do is turn it into something which is routine and mechanical. Drawings that are made to a formula will lack the essential element of originality, not only in the sense of your individual technique, but also regarding what you choose to draw and how it is interpreted. Ideally, each new drawing should be slightly different to the last, setting a fresh challenge and arousing your interest and motivation.

This is not to say that you cannot return to a subject or have a favourite theme. Indeed, it is possible to draw the same thing successfully over and over again, providing it continues to capture your imagination and offer something new each time you tackle it. What you must not do is stick to the same subjects simply because you fear failure, for this will seriously inhibit the opportunities to explore and experiment, which in turn will greatly restrict your development.

As for mistakes, it won't be long before you start to appreciate that they can actually point the way forward. Rather than seeing them only as a negative element of your work, you will find that you can in fact learn from your mistakes. As long as you are able to be self-critical and are willing to address the weaknesses in your drawing, then mistakes shouldn't matter too much. Refer to the relevant chapter of this book and, most importantly, practise and experiment.

Insight

Of course, acknowledge your mistakes and see what there is to learn from them. But don't feel that every mistake must somehow be corrected. Sometimes it is best to leave well alone or, at the other extreme, start a new drawing rather than struggle with something that is causing you big problems.

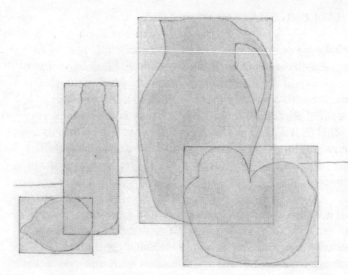

Illustration 1.7 A reliable way to start any drawing is to consider the basic shapes and proportions. Look at the space that each object occupies and the relative position of one object to another.

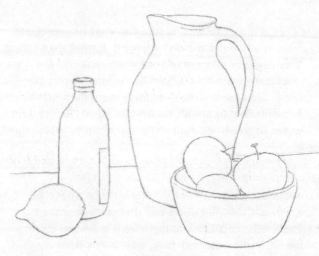

Illustration 1.8 Next, from the initial assessment of shapes and sizes, aim to create accurate outline shapes.

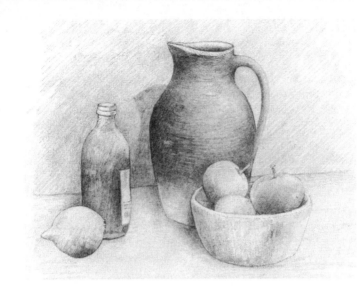

Illustration 1.9 Finally, add the necessary degree of tone and detail to make the drawing convincing. Pencil.

Exercises

1   *Start a drawing scrapbook. Keep in it any postcards and cuttings of famous drawings, photographs of subjects and ideas that appeal to you, and any other visual material which could inspire drawings. Aim for a wide choice of material. In time, this will form a very useful reference aid together with your notebooks and sketchbooks.*

2   *Next time you are near an art gallery, pop in and look at any drawings they may have on display.*

3   *Study the drawings in this section and note the different approaches, media and techniques used.*

4   *Now look carefully at the sequence of drawings in Illustrations 1.7–1.9. Choose a similar group of simple objects and try this exercise for yourself.*

10 THINGS TO REMEMBER

1 *People draw for different reasons, but essentially drawing is a means of expression and a method of contact between the artist and other people.*

2 *Drawing should also be enjoyable and satisfying.*

3 *There are lots of types of drawings, from plans and sketches to highly detailed studies.*

4 *As well, there are many different drawing media and techniques.*

5 *Initially, the best approach is to draw from observation – by looking at actual objects, landscape views and so on and aiming to make an accurate study of them.*

6 *Gradually, as you develop confidence, you will be able to draw with more individuality and expression.*

7 *Looking at drawings by other artists, particularly well-known artists, can be informative and inspirational.*

8 *Think of what you want to express in each drawing, and then decide on the best medium and technique to achieve this.*

9 *Don't be afraid to experiment or make mistakes.*

10 *The most successful drawings will convey just enough information while at the same time leaving something to the imagination of the viewer.*

2

....

Materials and equipment

In this chapter you will learn:
- *which materials you can use*
- *which materials you should start with*
- *how to experiment with different materials and explore their potential.*

_____

What can we use?

Unlike many art techniques, drawing does not need a lot of complicated equipment and expensive materials. In fact, most drawings can be made very simply. You will probably discover this when you are out somewhere, see a subject that you would love to draw, but do not have any obvious drawing equipment with you. In this sort of situation you have to be very inventive and make use of whatever is available. For example, I have made drawings on a brown paper bag, on a blank page at the end of a paperback book, on lined paper and even on a car parking ticket.

Most drawings are made with pencil on paper. Although this medium offers tremendous scope, don't be afraid to try as many other drawing tools and materials as you can. And remember, you don't necessarily have to draw with something that was specifically designed for drawing! As well as the more traditional shop-bought implements, there are plenty of unconventional ones, either found or home-made, that will give interesting effects. For example, you can add exciting textural effects to a drawing by using a cork or a comb dipped into some ink or paint. Similarly, you could draw with your finger or a stick that has been dipped into ink or paint, or use the same materials to create a spattered or stippled texture applied with an old toothbrush.

APPROPRIATE MATERIALS

The first step towards developing your drawing skills is to gain some experience and confidence with a wide range of drawing tools and materials. You will find information on pencils, charcoal, crayons, pens and inks in this chapter, with more detailed advice on coloured pencils, pastels and other colour techniques in Chapter 5. You will see many ways of using these materials in the illustrations throughout this book.

As you gain experience, you will notice that each medium has its particular strengths and characteristics, and that these in turn will help you create certain effects. Consequently, in time you will be able to choose the best medium for the type of drawing you want to make and, when appropriate, even combine a variety of media. Read through the whole of this chapter first and then study each drawing medium in more detail. Collect together as many different tools and materials as you can and test these out by completing the various exercises listed at the end of this chapter. You will be working with black and white techniques at first, but later, when you reach Chapter 5, there will be an opportunity to try out some ideas in colour.

Pencils

When you are buying pencils, always look for good quality graphite drawing pencils made by a well-known manufacturer such as Derwent, Faber-Castell, Stabilo or Staedtler. Pencils are marked to indicate their degree of hardness, which may range from 8B (softest) to 9H (hardest), with grades HB and F midway between the two. Very hard pencils – those in the 'H' range – are not normally suitable for general drawing. They cannot be handled with the same sensitivity as softer pencils and tend to indent the paper, thus making it difficult to erase lines that are wrong. Keep to a softer range to begin with. A selection comprising B, 2B, 4B and 6B is recommended, supplementing this with an HB if you need to make sharper, more defined lines or greyer and weaker tones.

One of the first things you will notice about pencils is that the character and tone of the marks are influenced by the pressure you apply. Naturally, some people work quite firmly and confidently, which means they are likely to create much bolder marks than someone whose approach is more restrained. You need to take this factor into account when you are buying pencils; consider the way that you work and choose your pencils accordingly. Ideally, you need a selection that will enable you to achieve a good balance of tones and lines, from very dark to very light.

Also, bear in mind that there can be subtle differences from one brand to another in the way that pencils respond – even though they are marked with the same degree of hardness. So, try out several brands and when you have found a type that handles well, keep to it. You will also find that the sort of paper you choose will influence the way that pencils and other materials respond, and consequently the effects that you can create.

Insight
Don't feel that you must always hold the pencil in the conventional way – in the same way that you would hold a pen for writing. As well, experiment with holding the pencil further up the barrel, or even right at the end. This will enable you to work with much freer lines and marks.

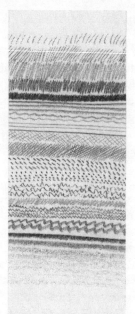

Illustration 2.1 Try this type of exercise to test out your pencils and see what lines and effects are possible.

WHEN TO USE PENCILS

Because it is so familiar to us, the ordinary pencil is often underrated as a serious drawing implement, yet it is one of the most versatile of all drawing media and the one that will most obviously reflect our drawing ability. Pencils suit everything from composition roughs to highly expressive drawings made on the spot. Use pencils for jotting down quick visual 'notes' and ideas as well as for problem-solving, analytical studies and reference sketches. Inexpensive and easy to use, pencils are certainly the best medium to start with. Another point in their favour is that they combine well with most other media, especially watercolour, inks and charcoal. Look at Illustrations 2.2–2.8 to see the sort of effects that are possible.

Insight

For broader pencil marks or for blocking in large areas of shading, hold the pencil in a more horizontal position, so that you can use the side of the pencil lead rather than the tip.

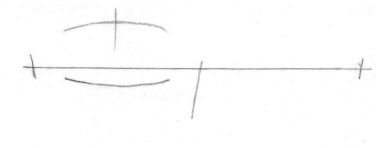

Illustration 2.2 When drawing an object like this, start by checking the relative height to width ratio.

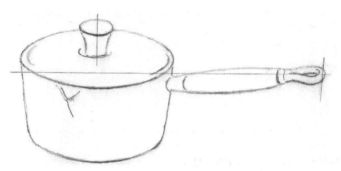

Illustration 2.3 As you draw the outline, vary the pressure on your pencil so that the nearer edges are stronger in tone.

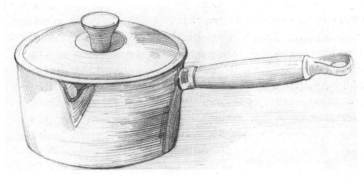

Illustration 2.4 You can suggest the three-dimensional form of the object by shading with lines, using heavier lines for the darker shadows. Note the source of light is from the left.

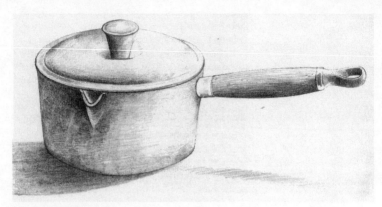

Illustration 2.5 Alternatively, you can work with a softer, darker pencil, blending the shading, as here. Note the source of light is from the right.

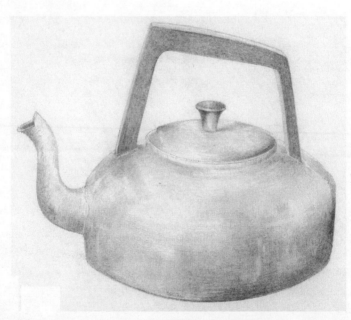

Illustration 2.6 You may need to use two or three different grades of graphite pencil to make a carefully resolved tonal drawing such as this.

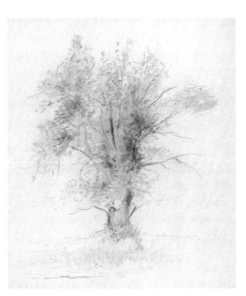

Illustration 2.7 This sketch was made with a carpenter's pencil, using both broad and thin strokes to create different effects.

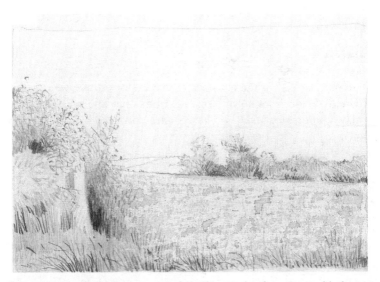

Illustration 2.8 Some graphite pencils are water-soluble. This means that, if you wet parts of the drawing with a brush and some clean water, you can create light wash effects, as in the foreground area of this drawing. Pencil and wax resist.

Modern pencils are manufactured from natural graphite that has been made into a paste by blending it in a powdered form with clay. The paste is then compressed and extruded into thin strips, which are subsequently dried and kiln-fired to make the leads. These are impregnated with waxes to make them draw smoothly, glued into a casing of soft wood, and finally finished with one or two coats of paint.

You can supplement your basic drawing pencils with wide carpenters' pencils, and graphite sticks, both of which are ideal for laying in very broad areas of tone and working on a larger, freer scale. Of course, you can also work in colour, using coloured pencils, water-soluble pencils and pastel pencils.

Insight

There are occasions when a blunt pencil is useful, but generally, and especially for details, a sharp point is best. To sharpen a pencil to exactly the sort of point or wedge shape you require, use a sharp craft knife rather than a pencil sharpener.

Charcoal

Charcoal was one of the first materials used for drawings. It was originally made from burnt twigs cut from vines and willow trees. Today, compressed sticks of charcoal are produced by firing willow rods in a kiln until the wood is carbonized. You can buy boxes of mixed thicknesses, from very thin to thick scene-painters' charcoal. A few sticks are always useful, especially for sketching and loose, large-scale work, as well as for creating greys, diffused shading effects and various textures and dabs of tone in conjunction with other drawing media.

As with any medium, it takes a little while to get used to charcoal and find the best way to create different line and tone effects. At first, there can be a tendency to press too hard and therefore apply too much medium. However, a little practice soon shows how much pressure is required to produce the necessary control and sensitivity with the charcoal marks. Essentially, charcoal sticks are quite brittle, and so must be handled with some care.

Because of its soft, sensitive quality and the fact that it can be smudged, blended and handled in many different ways, charcoal is a very versatile, expressive medium, especially for tonal work. When more positive lines and details are required, these can be added with charcoal pencils. Available in soft, medium and hard degrees, charcoal pencils can be sharpened to a point and, if used with moderate pressure, will respond just like graphite pencils.

As an introduction to using charcoal, break off a length of about 4 cm and try a few simple exercises. Hold the charcoal at various angles and apply different pressures to see what variety of lines and tones you can achieve. Try it on smooth paper as well as heavier quality paper and even coloured paper. Apply it sparingly at first and experiment with smudging it in different ways: with your fingers, a cotton bud, or a small piece of cloth or paper. You can also use the charcoal on its side for broad tones and general textures. Completed drawings will need spraying with fixative in the way described on page 183.

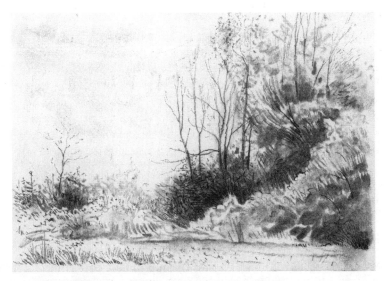

Illustration 2.9 A speedy, freely expressed location sketch drawn with charcoal.

Charcoal is an excellent medium for sketchbook work and getting a quick impression or feeling for the subject. Have a look at Illustrations 2.9 and 2.10. The sketch in Illustration 2.9 was made with a single stick of charcoal and shows the immediacy, liveliness and spontaneity of this useful medium. Contrastingly, for Illustration 2.10 I worked mainly with a charcoal pencil, using stick charcoal only for the general background tones. Charcoal also combines well with colour washes. Start with the main elements of the subject drawn in charcoal, and then add one or two colour washes made from diluted watercolour or ink and applied sparingly. For an example of this technique, see Plate 3.

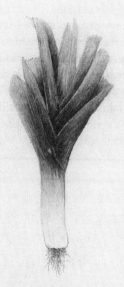

Illustration 2.10 Charcoal will give a wide range of tones and allow very subtle, blended effects. The medium also combines well with white chalk or pastel, which can be used for highlights.

Insight

A good way to add subtle, light tones to a charcoal drawing is to use an offsetting method. First, shade some charcoal onto a scrap piece of paper. Next, rub this with your finger and then rub your finger across the appropriate part of the drawing. Or you could use a putty rubber or a small piece of paper, instead of your finger.

Crayons

Both wax crayons and conté crayons are available in black, white and grey shades, which suit various tonal drawing techniques, and there is also a limited range of colours.

WAX CRAYONS

Wax crayons are inexpensive, and a box of assorted colours will make an interesting addition to your choice of drawing materials. As in Illustration 2.11, I sometimes draw with a sharpened black wax crayon, which can give surprisingly sensitive marks. Similarly, a black crayon is ideal for adding tones and textures in a mixed-media drawing, including offset textures using a rubbing technique.

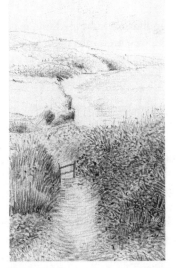

Illustration 2.11 As here, sharpened wax crayons can give surprisingly sensitive marks for conveying the sense of mood and atmosphere in a subject.

Rubbings

Rubbings work best on thin drawing paper. Choose a textured surface that matches the effect that you want to create in your drawing and place the relevant part of the drawing over the texture, which could be something like woodgrain, a metal grille or frosted glass. Then, using a short length of wax crayon on its side, shade over the particular shape or area. Apply light pressure to the crayon to begin with. If necessary, you can build up the strength of tone by shading across the area several times.

Resist textures

You can create other exciting texture effects by employing a resist technique, using a white wax crayon with India ink wash.

Coat the relevant part of the drawing with a thin layer of white wax crayon, or use an ordinary white candle. Paint over this with a light-tone wash made from a small amount of Indian ink mixed with plenty of water. As well, of course, you can make colour resist textures by using coloured wax crayons and watercolour washes.

CONTÉ CRAYONS

Conté was once a popular drawing medium, especially for figure studies. If you do some research into the history of drawing, you will find that a number of famous artists have used this medium extensively, notably Seurat.

Conté crayon is a hard, square-section, grease-free drawing chalk that is particularly successful on heavy quality paper. Like charcoal, it will give lines of great sensitivity as well as dramatic tonal effects. If required, sharpen the crayon to a point so that you can add fine lines and details to the drawing. Alternatively, for broad areas of tone and more expressive marks, work with a short length of conté crayon on its side. Conté pencils are also available. This medium will not smudge and consequently does not need spraying with fixative. See Illustration 2.12.

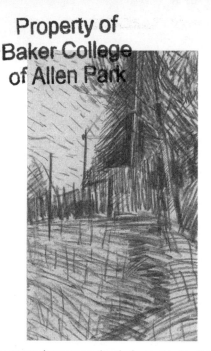

Illustration 2.12 This expressive drawing was made with a brown stick of conté. These crayons are most effective when used on a tinted paper with a slightly textured surface, as this brings out the character of the marks.

Pens

There are lots of different types of pens available today, each with its own character of line and range of techniques. Look out for mapping pens, script pens, technical pens (like Rotring and Faber-Castell), special art pens and sketching pens, cartridge pens, ball-point pens, brush pens and fibre and felt-tip pens. Dip pens, like mapping and script pens, will need some drawing ink. Other pens have their own built-in supply of ink or, as is the case with most technical pens, come with a replaceable cartridge of ink and interchangeable nibs. Additionally, you can experiment by making your own dip pens: sharpen sticks of wood or make a quill.

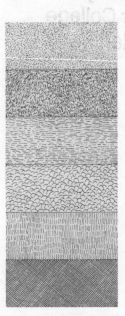

Illustration 2.13 A fine pen will give a huge variety of marks. Try this exercise for yourself.

You will find that dip pens tend to be the more unpredictable, since they do not have the controlled flow of ink that a reservoir pen has. Arguably, this gives scope for drawings of greater verve and personality, like the reed pen drawings of Van Gogh, for example. Again, it is a matter of trying out each kind of pen to see what lines and marks it will make, and in this way decide which pens suit you best. Remember also that the particular type of paper that you choose will influence the sort of marks and effects that are possible.

Many pen techniques are ideal for sketchbook work and quick studies. Look at Illustration 2.14, for example, which was made with a mapping pen, and the brush and ink drawing in Illustration 2.15.

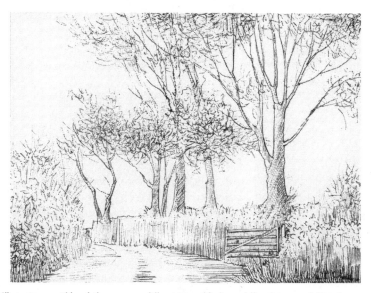

Illustration 2.14 Although there are many different types of fineline and fibre-tip pens available today, don't overlook the traditional dip pens. This drawing was made with a mapping pen and diluted Indian ink. Where fine lines are required, as here, try not to overload the pen or use it too vigorously – pressure and touch are all-important in creating lines of the correct strength.

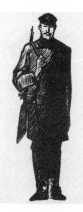

Illustration 2.15 With brush and ink you can create both lines and solid areas in your drawing.

Inks

You will find quite a few drawings in this book that have been made with Indian ink, sometimes diluted with water. The ink can be applied with a pen or a brush as specific, direct drawing, or with a brush or sponge for background wash and texture effects. Ink is also used in various spraying, spattering sgraffito and texture techniques. Additionally, you can buy coloured drawing inks, which will increase the range of possibilities, while thin ink washes are useful in a mixed-media approach, combined with work in pencil, charcoal or other media.

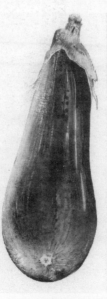

Illustration 2.16 You can vary an ink wash to give a variety of tonal strengths, and also scratch through the dry wash to create highlights. Pen and ink, with diluted ink wash.

Start with a small bottle of Indian ink as part of your basic stock of materials and use a dip pen or mapping pen to make a line drawing similar to the one shown in Illustration 2.14. Next, experiment with mixing some tonal washes, by adding a lot of water to one or two drops of ink. Test the ink washes on some scrap paper first, and then incorporate this technique into one of your pen drawings. See Illustration 2.16. For a more subtle and diffused wash effect, dampen the paper first.

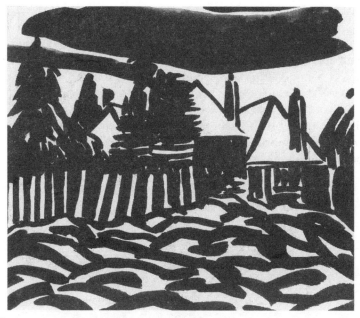

Illustration 2.17 This wonderfully bold, direct image was drawn with a brush and Indian ink.

Other drawing tools and materials

Drawing tools do not always have to be conventional. When you have mastered some of the basic techniques and started to make progress with drawing as a successful means of expressing your ideas, you may find that some rather unusual items help in the way you want to work. For example, as well as adapting and modifying tools like brushes and pens, you could try creating unusual textures and similar effects with an old comb or a toothbrush that has been dipped in some ink, or perhaps incorporating other offset techniques into your drawing.

Offset effects

Use the edge of a small piece of card, or a cork, a small sponge, the blunt end of a pencil or something similar, and dip it into some ink or paint. Now press the wet surface onto your drawing paper. Make a few test experiments first, and adjust the amount of paint or pressure as necessary. Introduce this technique into a pen drawing, or a brush or mixed-media drawing, where it will add the right type of texture or effect.

You can make interesting drawings by using items such as a spent ballpoint pen to indent marks into the paper. When these marks are shaded over with a soft 4B or 6B pencil they will show up quite clearly. For another unconventional technique, apply some small blobs of ink to a sheet of paper that has been propped up at a slight angle, and then blow these around, using a drinking straw blowpipe. The resultant sequence of random lines and shapes could be the basis for an abstract design perhaps, or it might suggest the starting point for an imaginary landscape or other idea.

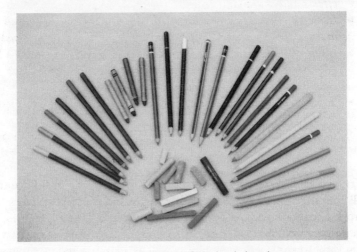

Illustration 2.18 A selection of pencils, wax crayons, soft pastels and oil pastels.

Paper

You will need a stock of good quality cartridge drawing paper.
The thickness and quality of paper is indicated by its weight in
grams per square metre (gsm).

Sheet sizes are now mostly standardized to ISO (International
Organization for Standardization) paper sizes. Each size in the list
below is exactly half of the next:

- ▶ **A4** *297 × 210 mm*
- ▶ **A3** *420 × 297 mm*
- ▶ **A2** *594 × 420 mm*
- ▶ **A1** *840 × 594 mm.*

The type of paper will greatly influence your drawing and the way
that different tools and media respond. The following papers are
recommended:

- ▶ *150 gsm cartridge paper will suit most pencil drawings,
  dry colour drawings in crayon and some ink techniques.*
- ▶ *180 gsm (or heavier) cartridge paper is best for very soft pencil
  effects and charcoal work.*
- ▶ *Use a smooth art paper, thin card, layout paper or non-bleed
  marker paper for work in pen and ink, fibre and felt-tip pens.*
- ▶ *Ingres papers, Canson Mi-Teintes paper and other pastel
  papers (in various colours) are the most suitable for chalks,
  pastels and heavier charcoal work.*
- ▶ *300 gsm watercolour paper is recommended for washes, brush
  drawings and tinted and painted work. It is also useful for
  charcoal and pencil drawings of subjects in which texture is an
  important quality.*

Try to collect samples of a wide range of different papers. Test out
all your drawing media on them to see which media and surfaces
work best. For some wet techniques the paper will need preparing
in the way described on page 150.

Paper is said to have a 'right' and a 'wrong' side, although in most cases either side can be used. Often, the preferable surface is the one with the less mechanical, even texture. To check this, hold the sheet up to the light and bend over one corner: one side will show an obvious, grid-like surface texture; the other will have a less mechanical, uneven surface.

Additionally, you will need a pocket-sized sketchbook in which to jot down day-to-day ideas and notes, and a larger, A4 sketchbook for more resolved drawings and studies, experiments with different media and techniques, composition roughs, and so on. There is more information on sketchbooks in Chapter 7.

Some sheets of tracing paper are also useful. You will find it cheaper to buy large sheets of paper and cut them down to size.

Insight

Avoid transporting or storing sheets of paper or finished drawings in cardboard tubes. Usually, once 'rolled', they are very difficult to get flat again, and perhaps in attempting this they will become creased and damaged. So, always store paper flat.

Erasers

There are several types of eraser, with each one serving a slightly different purpose. As erasers are inexpensive, it is well worth buying one of each type.

Kneadable (or putty) eraser

This is the best general purpose eraser. It works well with all media and surfaces, and will lift out and modify marks without scuffing, smudging or damage of any kind. It is particularly recommended for drawings made in charcoal and for any work on soft, fibrous papers, such as heavy quality watercolour papers. As the name implies, kneadable erasers are very malleable and are easily broken and shaped to suit the techniques you have in mind, whether erasing, blending, adding soft tones or creating highlights. For perfecting details, adding fine highlights, or similar effects, break off a small piece of the eraser and pinch it to form a point.

Plastic eraser
Use this for pencil drawings. It is not quite as versatile as a kneadable eraser, but again is very effective on most types of paper. Different sizes are available.

India-rubber eraser
This is the traditional, flexible eraser that artists have used for many years. It is made in a variety of shapes and sizes, including a very useful wedge-shape. While generally fine for making alterations to drawings on cartridge paper, it is not recommended for work on soft or obviously textured papers, as it may scuff the surface.

Rubber-tip pencil
Include this in your drawing equipment for adding small accents of light and tidying up details, as well as to draw 'in negative' by removing lines and shapes from solid areas of tone or colour.

Erasers can be an important drawing tool in their own right, and they will be especially useful when you are working with contrasts and subtleties of light and dark in drawings. Some eraser techniques are explained in Chapter 4.

Ancillary equipment

The following drawing aids and items of ancillary equipment are essential:

- *a sharp* **craft knife** *for sharpening pencils, cutting paper and so on*
- **fixative** *to spray on charcoal, pastel and any other finished drawings which are likely to smudge (choose ozone-friendly aerosol cans and use in well-ventilated conditions)*

- ▶ *a selection of* **clips and pins** *(use bulldog clips, drawing board clips or drawing pins to secure work while in progress)*
- ▶ *a plastic bevelled-edged* **set square** *or ruler*
- ▶ *a metal blowpipe* **diffuser** *for simple ink and paint spraying techniques*
- ▶ **paper tissues,** *cotton buds and cotton wool for modifying and blending soft media like charcoal and for various paint and texture techniques*
- ▶ *a roll of 5 cm brown* **gummed tape** *for stretching paper, as explained on page 150*
- ▶ *a* **drawing board.** *Proper art boards are expensive. Buy a sheet of 9 mm plywood which is slightly larger than an A2 sheet of paper. You can, of course, have smaller and larger boards as well.*

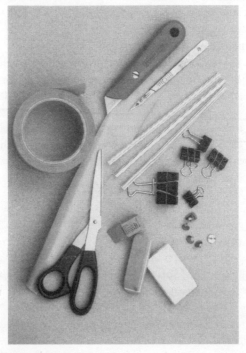

Illustration 2.19 Some useful drawing accessories.

See how your work progresses before buying any other equipment. For example, if you enjoy working outside you may eventually want to buy a sketching easel and folding stool.

Additionally, it is always useful to have a sturdy folio to keep your work in, or to be able to store it flat on shelves or in a plan chest.

Buying materials

Go to a reputable artists' materials shop where you should also be able to get some good advice and test out the samples and products you are interested in.

Here is a recommended 'starter' shopping list. You can add to this as the need arises:

- *ten A1 sheets of 150 gsm cartridge drawing paper – you can cut this to any shape and size you need*
- *two A1 sheets of 180 gsm (or heavier) cartridge paper*
- *a few sheets of buff, cream, and grey pastel paper*
- *two large sheets of 300 gsm watercolour paper*
- *an A4 spiral bound cartridge sketchbook*
- *a small notebook with smooth plain paper or a pocket-sized sketchbook*
- *HB, B, 2B, 4B and 6B drawing pencils*
- *a kneadable and a plastic eraser, and a rubber-tip pencil*
- *some water-soluble and coloured pencils – you can buy them separately, starting with just a few colours to try out*
- *a box of stick charcoal and a medium grade charcoal pencil*
- *a small selection of soft pastels (colours bought separately are cheaper than buying a whole box)*
- *a box of wax crayons*
- *a fine fibre pen (black); a marker pen (black) and a fine mapping pen*
- *a small bottle of Indian ink*
- *no.2 and no.4 watercolour brushes; a no.6 round hog brush*

▶ *one or two small tubes of gouache or watercolour paints – just buy red, yellow and blue to begin with*

▶ *the essential ancillary equipment listed on page 37.*

Testing out your equipment

Now that you have learned something about the range of drawing materials and have collected a stock of your own, it is time to do some testing and experiments. Drawings are often made for this reason – to explore ideas or try out different media and effects. As you work through the various chapters of this book, you will find that there are lots of occasions when it is useful to make roughs and preliminary sketches or test out different ideas and techniques before making the final decisions for the main drawing. This is a good habit to develop.

Keep all of your drawings for future reference and comparison. Although you may not want to show most of them to anyone else, they will prove very useful to you in demonstrating what progress you have made. Media tests and experiments should be labelled to identify which drawing tool or material was used, plus one or two brief notes on the effects you tried out.

Exercises

1   *Work through all the drawing media in your collection, starting with pencils. Using a new A3 sheet of paper for each medium, see what range of marks, shading effects and textures you can make. Try holding the drawing tools in different positions and using different amounts of pressure. Fill the sheets with notes and experiments in this way. Refer to Illustrations 2.1 and 2.13 to give you a starting point. Notice how, in Illustration 2.1, I have varied the angle and pressure of the pencil to see how this influences the character of the marks*

and lines, starting with the pencil held vertically and finishing with it used on its side; and how a variety of line effects, from wavy to hatched, can be achieved.

2   Now make one or two drawings of individual objects – see Illustrations 2.2–2.5. Start with the outline shape and then look at the main areas of light and dark in your objects. Try drawing them in several different media to see what effects are possible and which media work best.

3   Take as your subject a view from a window; try to find a view that is not too complicated. Start with a quick sketch in charcoal to get a 'feel' for the subject. Spend no more than ten minutes on this. Next, make a more resolved drawing in pencil. When you have finished, consider which drawing is the most successful, and why.

10 THINGS TO REMEMBER

1   Drawing is a very straightforward means of expression and all you need to start with is a pencil and a sheet of paper.

2   Pencils are surprisingly versatile as a drawing medium. They suit all techniques and types of drawing.

3   Charcoal is another inexpensive and very useful medium to try. It is particularly suitable for making quick sketches.

4   Remember that the type of paper will greatly influence your drawing and the way that different tools and media respond.

5   The other essential item for drawing is an eraser. For a good general purpose eraser, choose a kneadable (or putty) eraser.

6   Buy a sketchbook in which to jot down day-to-day ideas and notes.

7   Try as many different drawing media as you can. Before you consider working in colour, develop some confidence with the various black and white media discussed in this chapter.

8   Drawing tools do not always have to be conventional. You can invent your own tools and methods of working, such as drawing with a sharpened stick dipped in ink, or offsetting lines with a length of card.

9   Buy your materials in a reputable art shop where you can get advice and test out the items you are interested in.

10 Keep all your drawings for future reference and comparison.

3

Making a start

In this chapter you will learn:
- *how to make drawings with lines*
- *when to use guidelines*
- *how to draw with dots and other marks.*

Essential techniques

Now, from your initial experiments with various drawing tools and media, you should be able to move on to develop some confidence and skill with a number of basic drawing techniques. A knowledge of different techniques will mean that you can choose the most suitable method for your subject matter and the particular effects you want to create.

But first, let's clarify what is meant by technique. In fact, the term is ambiguous in that it can relate to both the general use of a medium as well as specific methods of handling that medium. For example, charcoal drawing is a technique, as is using hatching, stippling, or blending to apply the charcoal and create certain effects.

PRACTISE, PRACTISE!

The main techniques are line, tone, colour and texture. It is important to study these techniques very carefully and to practise every one until you feel confident about it. The illustrations offer some useful examples to work from and there are additional suggestions, tips and words of advice in the captions. Don't forget to try out the various techniques with as many different drawing materials as possible. This will give you a good range of basic skills from which to start developing your drawing ideas in a positive and individual way.

For most techniques, ordinary cartridge paper is fine, but occasionally you might also like to try a heavier quality paper such as Ingres paper or watercolour paper. Don't worry about wasting time or paper. All the time spent on drawing and experimenting is helping to develop your skills and understanding of the subject.

Insight

It is tempting to throw away unsatisfactory drawings, but in fact it is a good idea to keep them, certainly to begin with. They will help you judge how well your work is developing. Periodically, make a comparison between your most recent drawings and your early ones – noting where you have made progress and where you need to improve.

Drawing with lines

Line is the most commonly used drawing technique and the most versatile. Most drawing tools are designed to make lines. So you can use lines to show the shape of something, to create light and dark areas and textures, and to suggest different surface effects, like rippling water or windswept grass. Your lines can be delicate and sensitive or bold and expressive. They can be short or long, thick or thin, closely or widely spaced, curved, straight, ruled, freehand, and so on. A line drawing can be a quick sketch or a highly detailed study.

You may have explored some aspects of drawing with lines in the experiments and exercises recommended at the end of Chapter 2. If not, start by seeing what types of line are possible with each of your drawing tools and materials. Interesting media to try are hard and soft pencils, charcoal and charcoal pencils, pastel, fine fibre-tip pens, and a fine brush with some paint. Remember that the way you hold and work with the drawing tool or medium will affect the sort of lines you create. For instance, you will find that by using variations of pressure your lines will become thicker or thinner, lighter or darker. The type of paper you choose will also affect the sort of lines you can make. Try hatched lines, wavy lines, flowing lines, broken lines and so on.

Repeating lines

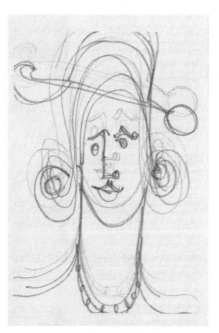

Illustration 3.1 This drawing was made with a pencil and fibre-tip pen held together – creating a kind of double-image effect.

The drawing in Illustration 3.1 was made by holding a pencil and a fibre-tip pen together. This created a sort of double-image effect. This is one of a number of ideas that are fun to try and at the same time will help you develop more confidence in using line techniques and handling different media. You might also like to try the following ideas, all of which work well in pen or pencil.

Using straight lines

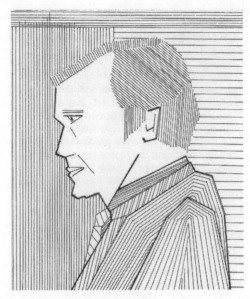

Illustration 3.2 You can use straight lines of different widths and directions to make a drawing, either with or without the help of a ruler. Pen and ink.

Look at Illustration 3.2. You can make drawings like this with a ruler or other form of straight-edge, or by drawing the lines freehand. Notice how the particular shapes and the illusion of space and form are achieved by using lines of different length, direction, strength and spacing.

Continuous line drawings
Try a drawing like the one shown in Illustration 3.3, which in fact was made from just a single, continuous line. This will certainly test your imagination and ingenuity! Start at the top and do not remove your pen or pencil until the drawing is finished – although you are allowed to backtrack over lines already drawn.

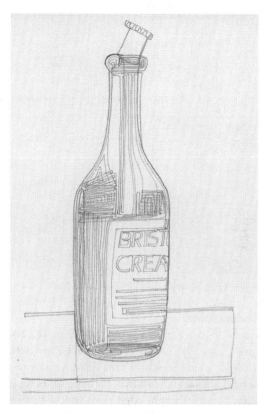

Illustration 3.3 Another useful technique to help you build up some confidence and control with the drawing medium, is to make a continuous line drawing, like this. Pencil.

Repeating outlines

Start with some bold outline shapes, and then repeat these outlines, inwards and outwards from the main shapes, as shown in Illustration 3.4. Leave a slight space between the lines – the closer the lines, the more intense the effect. Continue in this way until all the shapes, including the background areas, have been filled in.

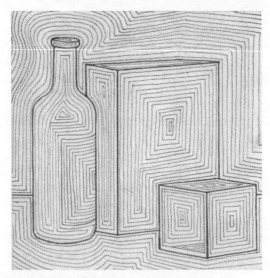

Illustration 3.4 This drawing was made by repeating the outline shapes. Pencil.

Impressed line drawings

Draw on a sheet of paper with a spent ball-point pen so that
the lines impress into the surface, although they are not actually
visible. Now shade over the whole area quite heavily with a very
soft pencil. The drawing will 'appear' as white lines against a
dark background. As well as being an interesting technique in its
own right, working with impressed lines can be a useful device in
dark-toned or well-resolved pencil drawings to create highlights or
textures, or bring out particular details.

CONTOUR DRAWINGS

In a contour or outline drawing you can use the economy of line to
great effect. By varying the thickness of line as well as its strength
(light/dark value), you can achieve the impression of something
three-dimensional. Thick bold lines will catch our attention, stand
out and appear nearer. In contrast, weak, thin lines recede and
give a sense of distance. There are many famous artists, including
Picasso, Matisse, Klee and Hockney, who have used this kind of
line technique.

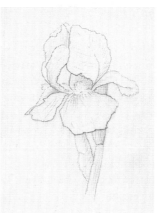

Illustration 3.5 Contour drawing. Pencil.

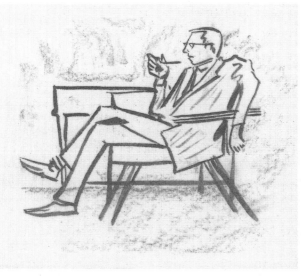

Illustration 3.6 Contour drawing. Brush and ink.

Contour drawing, as in the examples shown in Illustrations 3.5 and 3.6, is a splendid technique for sketchbook work and preliminary studies. The essence of an idea can be captured in a few, well-chosen lines, using variations of emphasis to suggest space and form. Try drawing different objects in your room in this way, perhaps in charcoal and fibre pen, as well as pencil.

VARIATIONS OF LINE

Surfaces can be modelled and different textures implied by using lines of various types and applying them with particular sensitivity and direction, perhaps involving more than one medium. Additionally, lines can suggest light and dark areas by varying their proximity. Notice how, in Illustration 3.7, the heavier, closely-spaced lines help create dark shadows, while the weaker, more open lines suggest highlights and soft tones. In this drawing the line technique is totally effective, for it combines both a sense of form and tone and something of the characteristics of the subject. Other ways of using line to convey tone are explained in the next chapter.

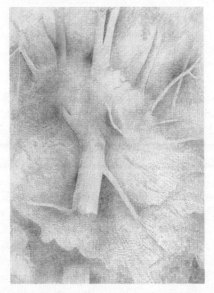

Illustration 3.7 By exploiting variations in spacing and intensity, hatched lines can convey different tonal values in a subject. Pencil.

Using guidelines

When you want to draw something very accurately it is usually a good idea to start with some faint guidelines to help position things correctly and get the right shapes and sizes. If you study the illustrations on the next few pages you will see how guidelines can be useful in creating a basic structure for the drawing. They provide a sort of skeleton, a starting point on which to build the accurate shapes. To work in this way you must first look at the subject matter in a very considered, analytical manner and decide which lines are the most important ones; which lines will provide the clues for the final drawing.

You might think that using construction lines, although aiding accuracy, will inhibit the work and give it a rigid, insensitive quality. Obviously this is a formal approach to drawing and worked as a step-by-step process it must, of course, hinder spontaneity and flow to some extent. However, there are many occasions in still life compositions and general planning where a few quick guidelines can aid the way forward, with subsequent work developed as freely as you wish.

Also, for beginners, it is sound practice to learn reliable ways of drawing cylindrical, symmetrical and similar basic shapes. Like perspective and other devices, once the theory of using guidelines is fully understood it will automatically influence the work without the necessity of going through all the stages.

Study Illustrations 3.8–3.17 and try out some of these ideas for yourself. For the present, concentrate on learning how to pick out the key lines within a drawing, and particularly focus on how this approach will help you draw important basic shapes, such as cylinder and other symmetrical shapes. Once you have mastered these basic shapes, you can apply the same procedure to more complex subjects. Incidentally, box shapes, which are very much influenced by perspective, are considered under this topic in Chapter 9.

CURVES, ELLIPSES AND CYLINDERS

Start by practising some curved lines, as shown in Illustration 3.8. Draw from inside the curve, with a free-flowing action of the hand.

If you are right-handed your curves will flow from left to right; if you are left-handed do the opposite. The action is from the wrist: try it with curves of different lengths and in different media. Think of an ellipse as a squashed circle. The degree to which it is squashed depends on your viewpoint: the higher your viewpoint, the more circular the ellipse.

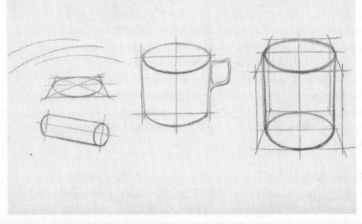

Illustration 3.8 Using guidelines to construct ellipses and cylindrical shapes.

Also in Illustration 3.8, notice how an ellipse can be constructed using a grid of lines. It actually fits into a square that is distorted according to your viewpoint and the influence of perspective. For this reason, the front half of the ellipse, being nearer to you, must be made slightly bigger than the back half.

Insight

A common mistake when drawing ellipses is to make the narrowest parts look rather 'pointed', rather than as part of the continuous flowing curve of a circle.

A good way to draw cylinders and similar shapes is to base them on a rectangle constructed to fit the estimated proportions of width to height. As in Illustration 3.8, use a central guideline to help ensure that the shape is balanced and to plot the ellipses. For a shape like a cup, start by constructing the main cylinder (the body) and then add other parts, such as the handle, to this. A common fault is to 'point' the ellipses at each side; instead, ensure that they are made from a continuous flowing line – with no abrupt changes of direction or acute angles. Remember that it is easier and more natural to draw from inside the curve, so turn your paper upside down to draw the nearer half of the ellipse.

For a cylinder or tube that is lying on its side, fix the centre lines, as shown in Illustration 3.8, and note that the basic rectangular shape is distorted by perspective as it recedes. These centre lines are also known as 'axis lines', particularly when they show the angle and direction of the basic shape, as here.

Insight

Keep your guidelines faint. Then they can easily be rubbed out or incorporated into the drawing.

SYMMETRICAL SHAPES

Many shapes are symmetrical – that is, equally balanced – or they are basically symmetrical with something added, like a handle. Once again, such shapes can be plotted either side of a central guideline. Begin with a rectangle based on the maximum width and height of the object. Put in a central line and draw one side of the shape. Notice where the shape changes direction and estimate such points in proportion to the whole. If you are right-handed, you will probably find it easier to draw the left-hand half of the shape first, and if you are left-handed, vice versa.

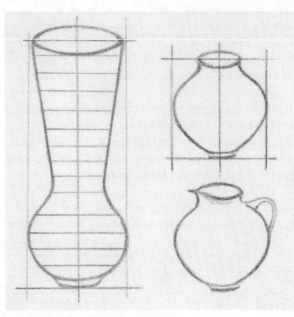

Illustration 3.9 Using guidelines for symmetrical shapes.

When you are satisfied with this, draw some guidelines across at key points where the outline alters. Now mark off a point on these lines that is the same distance from the centre as the corresponding point on the opposite side. Like the drawing in Illustration 3.9, create a series of these points which you can then join up to establish the other half of the shape. Rub out the unwanted faint guidelines and modify the main shape as necessary. Aim to practise all of the shapes in Illustrations 3.8 and 3.9 for yourself.

For other objects use as many or as few guidelines as seem necessary to help you build up an accurate outline. This general principle is demonstrated in the step-by-step drawings in Illustrations 3.10–3.13. From the basic framework you can construct a good outline drawing and then add detail and tone or colour.

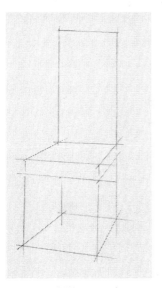

Illustration 3.10 Chair. Stage 1: Start with some guidelines to fix the main shapes and angles.

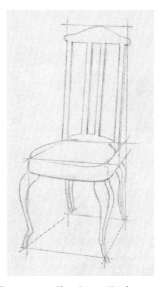

Illustration 3.11 Chair. Stage 2: Use the guidelines to make an accurate outline drawing.

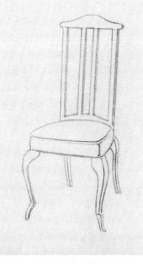

Illustration 3.12 Chair. Stage 3: Rub out the guidelines and perfect the outlines.

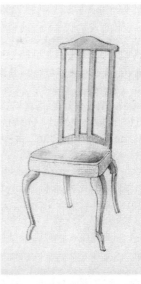

Illustration 3.13 Chair. Stage 4: Look at the object through half-closed eyes and notice the distribution of lights and darks. Add appropriate shading.

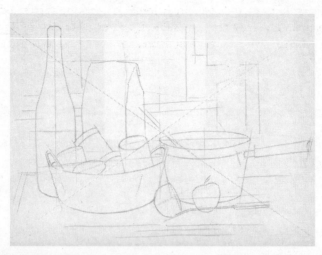

Illustration 3.14 Initial guidelines are particularly helpful when planning a more complex composition, both to help position the whole group on the sheet of paper and to fix the position of individual shapes in relation to each other.

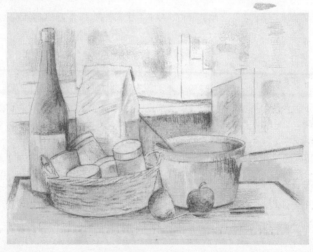

Illustration 3.15 Keep any initial guidelines faint, so that they are easily rubbed out and will not interfere with the way the drawing is developed. Charcoal and wash.

Initial guidelines are especially helpful when planning a still life drawing, like the one shown in Illustrations 3.14 and 3.15. Here you need to fix the particular scale of the work before defining the position and shape of each object and its overall size relative to the others. In fact, guidelines are helpful for checking angles and proportions when drawing any subject, and they are especially useful when drawing the human figure, as demonstrated in Illustrations 3.16 and 3.17.

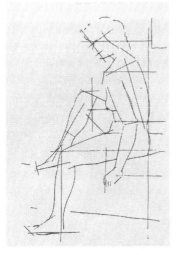

Illustration 3.16 Life study. Stage 1: working with guidelines to help fix the pose and proportions.

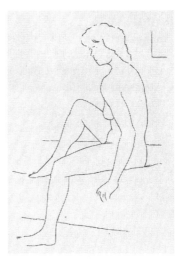

Illustration 3.17 Life study. Stage 2: erase the guidelines to leave an accurate outline shape to work from. Fibre pen.

Insight

Guidelines are a good supporting mechanism initially and will help you build up some confidence in drawing a wide variety of shapes. However, in time you will find that you can do without most of the guidelines and instead perhaps use just one or two small marks to help you plot the position of things.

Negative shapes

As well as using guidelines in the manner described, looking at the background areas or 'negative' spaces around them can help in constructing accurate shapes. The gaps in and around the subject you are drawing will often help in observing and understanding it. So, as a further check when you are drawing a particular object, refer to the spaces around it to help you define it more clearly. See Illustration 3.18.

Insight

Sometimes there is no need to actually draw the outline (or part of the outline) of something, but instead make use of the way that a contrasting dark background shadow or similar effect will define the shape for you. This effect is known as 'counterchange' – using dark shapes against light, or vice versa.

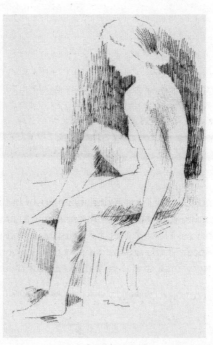

Illustration 3.18 Remember to consider the background shapes and 'negative' spaces. These are other important factors that will help you create accurate outlines. Fibre pen.

Drawing with point

Lines are one way of making marks. Another good method is to use dots or 'stabs' of tone or colour. Soft pencils and most pens are suitable for this technique, especially fine, fibre-tipped pens, ball-point pens, art pens, and technical pens which use interchangeable nibs of various thicknesses. Hold the pencil or pen vertically and pounce it up and down to produce a sequence of dots. Alternatively, hold it at a slight angle if you want to achieve little stabs of tone.

You can create contrasts of light and dark by varying the pressure on the pen or pencil. Also, of course, by combining different drawing tools you can exploit variations in the size and texture of the dots, although it is best to do a few tests first to check how successful this might be. Some pens use a much more intense ink than others. Equally, interesting effects are possible by working with a range of coloured pencils, the softer conté pencils generally proving the most suitable. Through your experiments with this technique, you will also find that you can make dots and dashes by other means: for example, by offsetting marks from a drinking straw, a thin piece of dowel or the blunt end of a paintbrush that has been dipped in ink.

Making a drawing entirely with dots is obviously a time-consuming and somewhat repetitive process. On the other hand, the broken texture and different tone effects are unusual and visually very interesting. This is a method that is particularly good for exploring subtle variations of light and dark, as in the woodland study in Illustration 3.19. Here I used a fine fibre-tip pen, varying the pressure on the pen and the spacing between the dots to create the tonal contrasts.

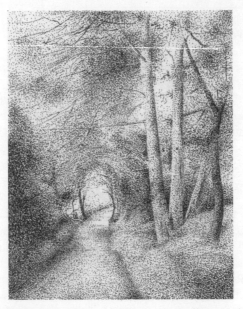

Illustration 3.19 Drawing with point. This drawing was made with a fine fibre-tip pen, holding it vertically and pounding it up and down to produce a sequence of dots. By varying the pressure on the pen and the spacing of the dots, you can create contrasts of light and dark areas.

Choose point techniques to suit a particular purpose in your drawing; you may decide that you need to combine several different techniques to achieve the effects you want. Point techniques are usually best for suggesting an uneven or textured surface, subtle effects such as a reflection in glass or water, faint outlines, or light to dark shadows. Also, as in many of the drawings by Van Gogh, Signac and Seurat, point combines well with linear and other techniques. See Illustration 3.20.

Outlines formed from a series of dots are less rigid and precise than those made as a continuous, solid line, making the mood or feeling of the drawing softer and freer. When deciding which point technique to use, think of the effect you want to suggest and try to match it up with one of the methods listed below. Remember that you will need to choose a type of paper to suit the media and techniques you have in mind.

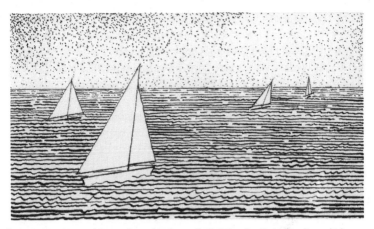

Illustration 3.20 Lines and dots can be combined very effectively in a drawing, as here. Pen and ink.

Try these different point techniques:

- ▶ **Pencils** – *Various types of pencil are suitable, but softer pencils such as 4B and 6B will give the most successful results. Charcoal pencils are also useful. Vary the pressure on a soft pencil to give contrasting light and dark effects.*
- ▶ **Pens** – *Use fibre-tip, ball-point or technical pens. If you combine a fine pen with a thicker pen, this will increase the range of effects that are possible. Don't press too hard or you will damage the nib or point of the pen.*
- ▶ **Dowel** – *You can make larger dots by dipping the end of a round pencil into some ink and pressing this down onto your drawing. This method is known as offsetting, and it can be used to create pattern effects in your drawing or areas of heavy texture. You can cut short lengths of round wood or dowel especially for this purpose. Used in the same way, drinking straws will give an open texture that can be very interesting and effective.*
- ▶ **Stipple** – *Use a stiff-haired round hog brush or a special stippling brush for this technique. Dip the brush into some ink or paint and offset it by stabbing it up and down on your paper. Use just a little ink or paint on the brush.*

▶ **Spray and spatter** – *Sprayed areas make good backgrounds and textures and combine well with pen and ink drawing. Use a spray diffuser with some drawing ink or alternatively try using an old toothbrush dipped into some ink or paint. Hold the brush directly in front of the part of the drawing you want to spatter and pull back the bristles with your forefinger. As the bristles spring back they will shower the drawing with fine spray. If you want to keep the spatter to a limited area then you will need to protect the rest of the drawing with some scrap sheets of paper.*

Exercises

1 *Refer to Illustrations 3.5 and 3.6, and try some contour drawings of your own, perhaps of a telephone, an upright chair, a bunch of keys or a lace-up shoe. Choose a different medium for each drawing.*

2 *Put together a still life group consisting of three or four kitchen objects. Select them carefully to give a variety of shapes and sizes and arrange them into an interesting composition. Look at Illustration 3.14. Starting with some guidelines, make a line drawing on an A3 sheet of paper to show the accurate shape and position of each object. Next, add more detail and consider the main light and dark effects, as in Illustration 3.15. Work in pencil or charcoal.*

3 *Make some experiments in your sketchbook using a variety of drawing tools to produce a range of point effects, from very small and faint dots to large and bold ones. Try coloured pencils and pastels as well as ordinary pencils and pens.*

4 *Study the method used in Illustration 3.19 and make a similar drawing using point techniques. As reference for your drawing you could use one of your own sketches or photographs, or you could work from direct observation of the subject matter. For example, you could make a drawing of part of your garden, or of a view in your local park or in the countryside somewhere.*

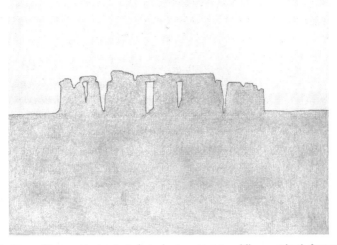

Illustration 3.21 If you want to spray part of your drawing using a spray diffuser or airbrush, first you need to cut a paper template to mask out the area or areas that you wish to protect from the spray, as in the top part of this illustration. Apply the spray lightly, allowing it to dry before re-spraying, and so build up the effect you require. Diluted Indian ink applied with a spray diffuser.

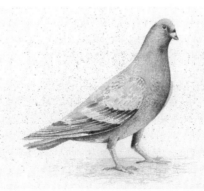

Illustration 3.22 This drawing was made on watercolour paper to suit the various ink and wash techniques that were used. Note the texture for the ground area. This was made with a hog hair brush dipped in just a little ink, so that when it was dragged across the paper it just caught the surface, creating a broken, 'dry-brush' texture.

3. Making a start 63

10 THINGS TO REMEMBER

1   *The main drawing techniques are line, tone, colour and texture.*

2   *The term 'technique' also applies to the general use of a medium (pencil, charcoal, conté and so on) as well as specific methods of handling that medium (hatching, stippling, blending and so on).*

3   *Line is the most commonly used drawing technique. Lines can be drawn with most drawing tools and materials.*

4   *Use variations of pressure to create lines of different strength and intensity.*

5   *Lines are very versatile: they can be used to suggest three-dimensional form, tone, texture and surface characteristics.*

6   *Linear techniques are particularly good for contour drawings, sketches, preliminary studies and composition roughs.*

7   *You can combine lines with any other technique.*

8   *When you want to draw something very accurately, start with some faint guidelines to help position everything correctly and get the right shapes and sizes.*

9   *Also, to help construct accurate shapes, check the background areas or 'negative' spaces around them.*

10 *Use point techniques (dots or 'stabs' of tone or colour) when you want to suggest an uneven or textured surface, subtle effects such as reflections in glass or water, faint outlines, or light to dark shadows.*

4

....

Light and dark

In this chapter you will learn:
- *how to judge the different light and dark values in a subject*
- *how to choose appropriate shading techniques*
- *when to use an eraser.*

Form and space

Certainly to begin with, in most of your drawings you will want to convey a good likeness of something. Invariably, when working towards this type of result, one of the main challenges is how to make things look three-dimensional. As drawings are made on a flat, two-dimensional sheet of paper, artists have to employ various devices to create the illusion of space and depth. Working with contrasts of light and dark, or in other words different tonal values, is one way of doing this.

The first step towards understanding tone is to observe and consider the way that light plays on different objects, creating a whole range of effects from deep, dark shadows to glinting highlights. These variations of light and dark help to describe the form of the object and consequently make it look curved, undulating, square or whatever. To interpret the different tonal values effectively, you will need to learn about shading techniques and how to choose the best method for the subject matter and quality of light that you are dealing with.

Shading techniques

Each drawing medium or tool will produce its own distinctive range of tone and particular tonal characteristics. With some, like felt-pens, the extent of tonal variation is limited, while with others, like charcoal or soft pencil, there can be an extensive range, from subtle lights to intense darks. Generally, variations of tone are achieved by altering the pressure applied to the drawing medium. Get used to handling different media in this way so that you know what tonal effects they can give.

In some of your drawings, you might need to combine several drawing tools or media in order to create the right contrasts in tone and surface characteristics. When you are drawing in pencil, for example, you will probably have to use several different degrees of pencil (perhaps a 4B, 2B and HB) in order to achieve a good range of tones.

Start by practising the various shading techniques demonstrated in Illustrations 4.1 and 4.2. Try the same sequence of exercises, then see if you can find other ways of creating tonal variations, perhaps using different media. As always, remember that the type of paper is important: use cartridge paper for pencil work, a smooth art paper for fine pens, and a heavier quality paper (Ingres, watercolour, etc.) for charcoal. Your exercises could include the following techniques:

▶ **Hatching** – *Use short, crisp lines at an angle of about 45 degrees. Notice how the spacing and strength of the lines determines the intensity of the tone.*

Illustration 4.1 A tonal strip. Make one of these to help you assess the strength and variety of tones in the different subjects you want to draw. Use a 3B or 4B pencil and, starting with light pressure, gradate the tone from very light to very dark, as shown. Hold the strip up to the subject you are drawing and match each part to its corresponding tone on the strip.

Illustration 4.2 There are various ways of creating tone with a soft pencil: hatching; cross-hatching; using the lead of the pencil on its side to create an even tone; varying the pressure to make a dark to light effect; and creating a smooth, even tone by rubbing the pencil into the surface of the paper with a small piece of paper.

▶ **Cross-hatching** – *Work as for hatching, then cover with a series of lines in the opposite direction. This creates a more solid tone effect.*

▶ **Linear tone** – *You can shade with a series of straight lines. The spacing and strength of the lines is important. Thin, faint lines will suggest a light area of tone, while bolder lines placed closer together will produce a dark tone.*

▶ **Pressure** – *Use a soft pencil (3B–6B). Hold the pencil almost horizontally, so that the side of the lead is used. Start with very heavy pressure and gradually reduce this so that your shading goes from very dark to light. Try to achieve this without any obvious gaps or lines.*

▶ **Blending** – *You can use a soft pencil, charcoal or pastel for this technique. For a subtle effect, work the tone into the surface of the paper by gently rubbing it with your finger or a small piece of paper or cloth.*

▶ **Shading and erasing** – *For highlights, like the reflections on glass or water, shade all over the area first and then lift out lines and patches with a clean, pointed piece of rubber. If necessary, cut a thin slice from an eraser to use for this purpose. Putty rubbers and other soft erasers can also be used for blending. Eraser techniques are covered in more detail on page 73.*

▶ **Charcoal** – *For small areas, hold and use the charcoal like a pencil. For bigger areas, use a short length of charcoal on its side. Do not press too hard or the charcoal will break. You can blend charcoal in the manner described above.*

▶ **Pen** – *Fine pens will suit line techniques such as hatching, point and other ideas, like the scribbled tone effect shown in Illustration 4.3.*

> **Insight**
>
> Although you can achieve many different shading effects with a soft pencil (a 3B or 4B), do try charcoal and pen and ink as well if you can. And remember to keep all of your practice exercises for future reference.

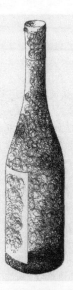

Illustration 4.3 You can use all sorts of methods to suggest variations of tone. Note the scribbling technique used here, made with a fine fibre-tip pen.

Tonal key

When you are drawing something from direct observation, begin by making a careful assessment of the source and direction of light, and consequently the extent and distribution of shadows and the general tonal 'key' of the subject. It could be that your subject is evenly lit and therefore there are few darks of any significance. Alternatively, a strong light from a particular direction will cause positive shadows and perhaps many variations of tone. Draw a simple object to try out these differences. See Illustration 4.4.

With tone, as with many aspects of drawing, the process usually works best if it is simplified. If you half close your eyes it will help you identify the main light and dark areas. To begin with, think in terms of three main tones: dark, medium, and light. Avoid overshading. In general, use the white of the paper as the lightest tone and try to achieve some good contrasts between this and the darkest areas. Now make a drawing that restricts tone in this way, like the still life in Illustration 4.5.

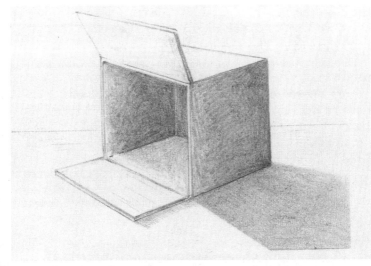

Illustration 4.4 In all your drawings it is important to note the source and direction of light. This will help you understand the different tonal values involved and place the shadows. Pencil.

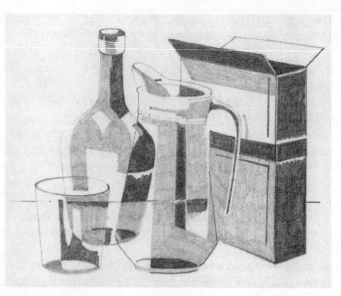

Illustration 4.5 Use the white of the paper as the lightest tone and begin to think in terms of three main tones: dark, medium and light. Pencil.

In some drawings, short, hatched strokes are the best choice and will convey something of the character of the subject matter as well as depicting the different tones. In other drawings, you may need to work with a combination of linear tone and blended tone, as demonstrated in Illustrations 4.6–4.8.

Insight

Don't attempt to include every subtle variation of tone in your drawing: it will make the process and in fact the drawing too complex. On the other hand, if the subject you have chosen is fairly even-toned, exaggerate the contrasts to add to the impact of the drawing.

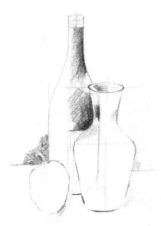

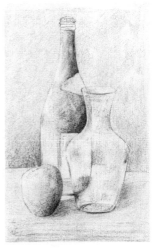

Illustration 4.6 Still life drawing.
Stage 1: Define the principal shapes.

Illustration 4.7 Still life drawing.
Stage 2: Apply general areas of tone.

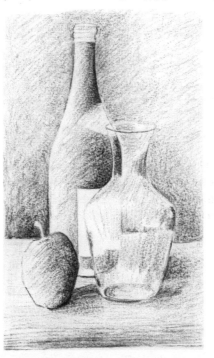

Illustration 4.8 Still life drawing. Stage 3: Work over the drawing with a putty eraser to modify the tonal contrasts, model forms and create highlights. Charcoal and charcoal pencils.

SHAPE FIRST!

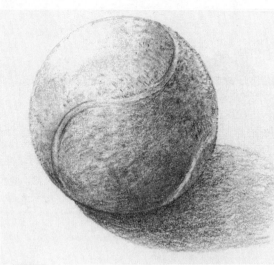

Illustration 4.9 Exploiting variations of pressure to create different tones. Pencil.

Tone and shape work together to give us a true likeness of
something. Sometimes, when we look at an object, the shape is not
that clear, perhaps because of the huge range of tonal values and
textures that cover it. Nevertheless, look for the shape first, and
plot this as accurately as you can before tackling the modelling and
detail. Once you have a satisfactory shape to work with, consider
carefully which shading techniques will be most suitable. The
drawings in Illustrations 4.9 and 4.10 combine various shading
methods: solid tone, variations of pressure, blended tone and
erased highlights.

Insight

Do just enough shading to bring out the form and character
of the subject. Avoid overworking the drawing and thus
spoiling its freshness and appeal.

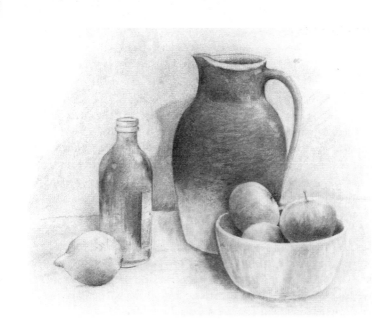

Illustration 4.10 Still life study worked in charcoal and involving a variety of techniques to convey different tonal and texture effects.

Erasers and tone

As well as being a useful means of correcting mistakes in a drawing, erasers can be used much more creatively, especially when you are working with tone. With the right eraser and technique you can quickly add to the interest, vitality, movement, atmosphere and other qualities involved in interpreting an idea. Indeed, whatever the circumstances and approach, it is far better to view erasers as contributing positively to the development of a work, rather than seeing them only in a negative context – simply as a way of eradicating a mistake.

Insight

Try to use an eraser as little as possible for correcting mistakes. If you get to rely on an eraser to put things right,

(Contd)

this will seriously impede your progress and your ability to draw with confidence and expression. Occasionally, try some drawings for which the eraser is banned!

Although sometimes it is necessary to use a vigorous rubbing action to erase part of a drawing completely, on other occasions a soft dabbing technique might be all that is required to weaken a tone or fade an outline. The sharp corner of an eraser is ideal for lifting out a small accent or highlight from a dark tone while, used against a straight-edge, a plastic eraser will give a really crisp edge or outline to the selected tonal area.

In contrast to a conventional drawing, where the strongest tones are built up gradually while preserving the light areas, by placing more emphasis on the use of the eraser you can work the other way round. Try beginning with the dark tones and then using a soft eraser to take out the lightest parts. This works particularly well with drawings made in charcoal, pastel or soft pencil.

ADDING HIGHLIGHTS

The smaller wedge-shaped rubbers are very useful for working into an area of tone or colour to create flecks of light, small highlights, or slightly softer, contrasting passages. Held quite vertically and using just the sharp edge of the wedge-shape, this type of eraser is ideal for adding accents of light to water, for example. Swiftly pull the eraser in a horizontal direction to lift out fine lines and other marks. Another advantage of the wedge-shaped edge is that it allows you to 'draw' with the eraser and tidy-up and lift out quite precisely up to a clearly defined outline. Alternatively, you can use the whole width of the eraser, lightly dragging it across an area to soften the tone.

Refer to page 36 for information on the different types of erasers, and check out the eraser techniques used in Illustrations 4.9 and 4.10.

Here are some tips for using erasers:

▶ *Keep your eraser clean by occasionally rubbing it on some scrap paper to offset any accumulated graphite dust and similar deposits. If a plastic or India-rubber eraser gets really dirty, you can trim back the edge with a craft knife.*

▶ *To make really fine 'negative' lines and highlights, break off a small piece from a putty eraser or cut a small slither from an India-rubber or plastic eraser.*

▶ *When you modify a dark tone in one area, the eraser will pick up a certain amount of medium, and you can take advantage of this by dabbing the eraser up and down or dragging it across another part of the drawing where you require a light tone or texture.*

Exercises

1 *Find an interesting old building in your locality and make several tonal studies of it in your sketchbook. Begin by half-closing your eyes to help you assess the various tones involved, and refer to the tonal strip shown in Illustration 4.1. Try different viewpoints and details, making some drawings in pencil and some in charcoal.*

2 *Make a pencil drawing of a basket and some items of shopping from a supermarket. Concentrate on constructing accurate shapes and suggesting the three-dimensional form of each object through the use of tone, employing a variety of techniques. Ignore details such as lettering, patterns and decorative designs.*

10 THINGS TO REMEMBER

1 *Tone is the use of light and dark contrasts in a drawing.*

2 *Working with tone helps to create a true likeness of something and express its three-dimensional form.*

3 *To help judge the tonal values in the subject you have chosen, look at the way the light plays on the different surfaces, creating a whole range of effects from deep, dark shadows to glinting highlights.*

4 *The overall impression of the tonal values in a subject is known as the 'tonal key'.*

5 *Usually, to create an effective drawing, you may have to simplify or exaggerate the tonal contrasts.*

6 *You can get a good idea of the main tones to concentrate on by looking at the subject through half-closed eyes.*

7 *Start with the shapes and then model the tones.*

8 *There are various techniques for drawing with tone which are appropriate to different media and drawing tools. Hatching and blending are the main techniques.*

9 *In general, variations of tone are achieved by altering the pressure on the drawing tool or medium.*

10 *Remember also that you can use an eraser for modifying areas of tone and lifting out highlights.*

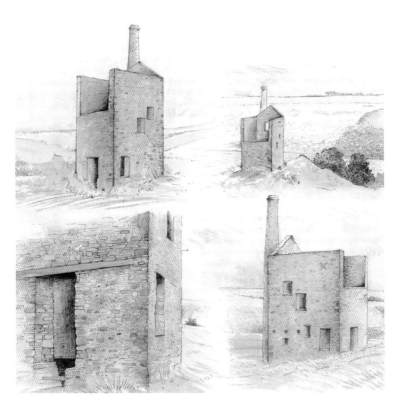

Plate 1 Location studies made with pencil and colour wash.

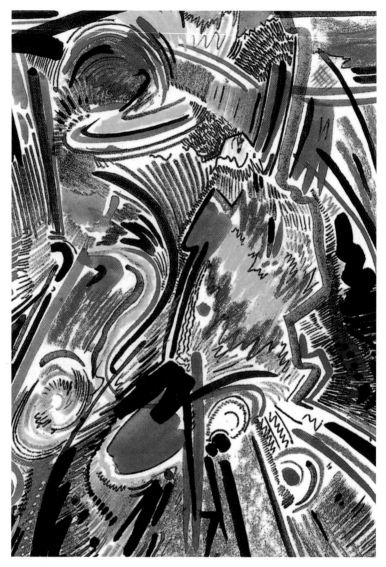

Plate 2 Various media have been combined in this freely expressed abstract drawing, including coloured pencils, pastels, inks and felt-tip pens.

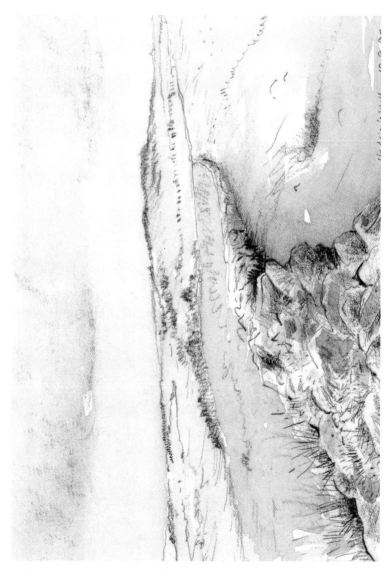

Plate 3 A quick, on-the-spot colour sketch like this is fun to make and will prove ideal reference information for a more resolved studio drawing later on. *Charcoal and wash*.

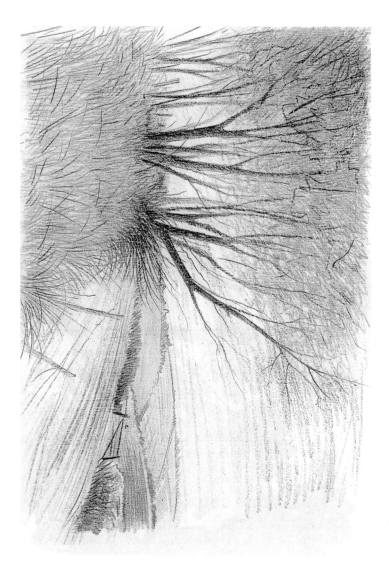

Plate 4 The way the marks are applied, particularly the direction of the pencil strokes, gives a sense of form and energy to the drawing. *Coloured pencils.*

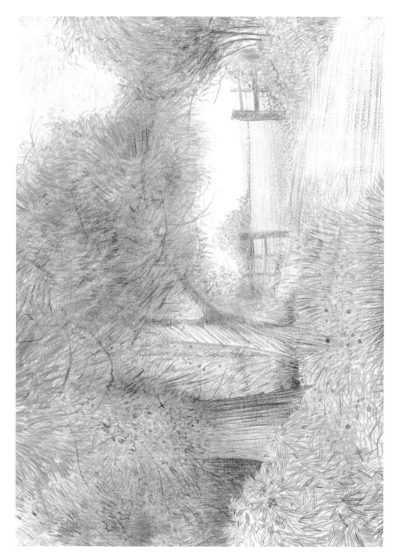

Plate 5 The surface of the paper can play an important part in creating the kind of effects you want. This landscape study was made on watercolour paper that had a slightly rough surface and consequently this enhanced the textural qualities in the drawing. *Coloured pencils*.

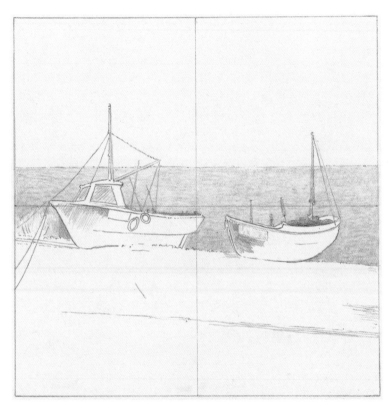

Plate 6 Fishing boats. Stage 1: Planning the composition and carefully drawing in the main shapes.

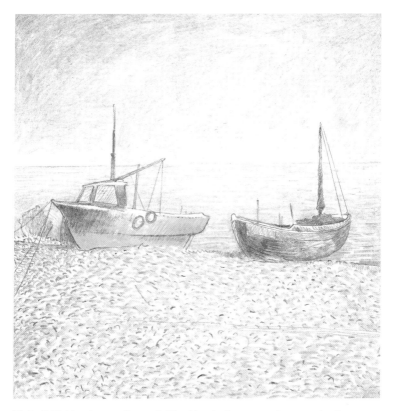
Plate 7 Fishing boats. Stage 2: Blocking in the general areas of colour.

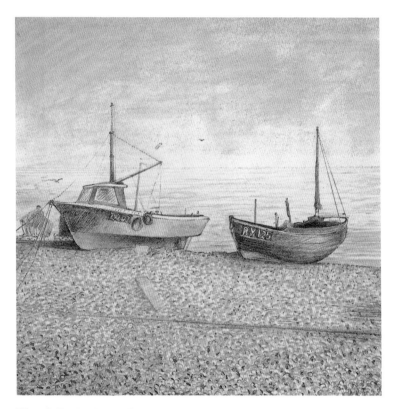

Plate 8 Fishing boats. Stage 3: Refining the colour and adding the necessary detail. *Graphite and coloured pencils.*

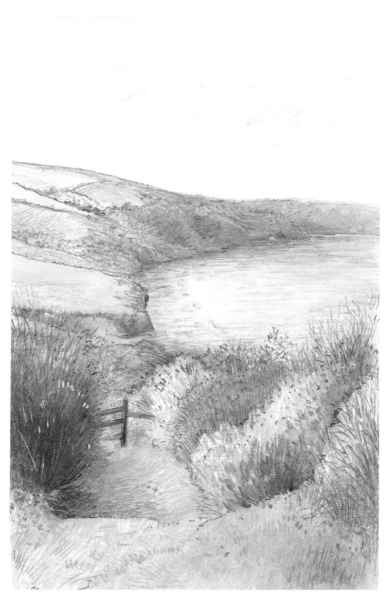

Plate 9 Ordinary coloured pencils can be combined with water-soluble coloured pencils to create a greater variety of dry colour and wash effects, as in this landscape drawing.

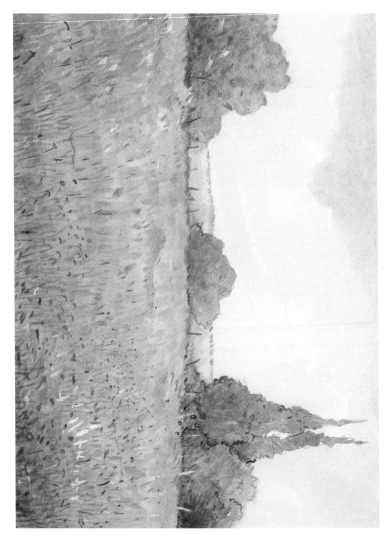

Plate 10 If required, with water-soluble pencils you can achieve quite a painterly quality, as here.

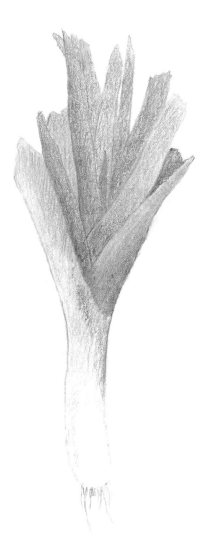

Plate 11 Leek study. Stage 1: Making the basic drawing with dry colour.

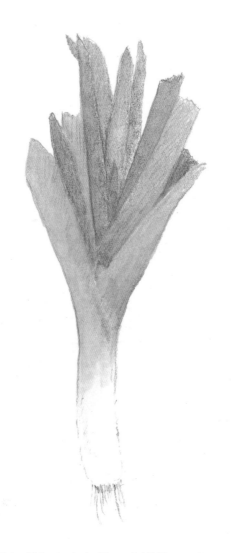

Plate 12 Leek study. Stage 2: Wetting and blending the colours, using a soft brush with some clean water.

5

....

Drawing in colour

In this chapter you will learn:
- *which media are best for colour work*
- *how to use different colour techniques.*

Colour and subject matter

Everyone who draws is involved with colour because in the
first instance, this is how we see the subject matter – in terms of
coloured shapes. We look at the subject before we can make any
decisions about the best medium and techniques to use to represent
it. Observation is important, not just to notice the actual colours,
but also to see how colours interact and create the effects and
sensations that characterize the subject matter. Thereafter, the
method of interpretation is influenced by individual skills and
modes of expression.

With colour, of course, you can adopt an entirely representational
approach and choose to reproduce the colours faithfully as seen,
as in Plate 1. Or you can work in a much freer way based on your
personal feelings and responses, as in Plate 2. When making the
initial assessment, try to view colours without any preconceptions,
as if you were seeing the objects for the first time. For example, in
a landscape it is very easy to assume that a field or grassy bank is
just a patch of green, whereas a close analysis might show that the
colour content is actually much more exciting and varied.

Also you will find that, if used in their raw state, some colours can be quite intense. You can reduce this effect by using the colours in a weaker form (in the case of coloured pencils and pastels by applying less pressure or, with inks, by diluting the colour with water), by mixing the colour with another colour, or by applying the colour over a pre-tinted surface. Generally, drawings are more effective if the colour palette is restricted in some way, and thus you keep to perhaps just five or six colours. The range of colour media includes coloured pencils, pastels and inks.

Coloured pencils

As well as traditional coloured pencils, designed for dry colour work, you could also try water-soluble coloured pencils and pastel pencils. Made from high quality coloured pigments, these pencils have an acceptable lightfast quality and offer a composition and consistency that allows immense versatility in their use. The range of available colours is now extensive – up to 120 in some brands. Coloured pencils are particularly good for portraiture and still life studies, and also for quick visual 'notes', composition roughs and reference drawings and sketches.

HANDLING CHARACTERISTICS

The colour intensity and handling characteristics of coloured pencils can vary tremendously from one brand to another. To find a range of pencils that suits the way you like to work, try experimenting with a small selection of colours from several brands. The hardness of the colour strip is the key aspect to check: pencils with a hard colour strip can be sharpened to a fine point, which is perfect for controlled lines and layered hatched effects, whereas softer leads are better for smudging and blending.

One of the first things you notice when working with coloured pencils is that they are very sensitive to the pressure applied, and this is something to exploit in your drawings. Firm pressure results in bold marks and intense colours, while light pressure gives more subtle effects.

The way you hold the pencil will also influence the type of mark that is possible. Usually, for controlled and detailed work it is best to hold the pencil quite near the tip. But for broader strokes and a freer, more expressive approach, hold the pencil about half-way up the barrel and use it at more of an angle. Another factor that influences the character of the drawing is the choice of paper. Choose a smooth surface, such as a heavy quality cartridge paper, when you want to focus on well-defined shapes, precision and detail using dry colour techniques. For drawings made with water-soluble pencils or for a more textural, broken colour effect, a Not or Rough surface watercolour paper is the best option.

Insight
Start with just a few coloured pencils and buy individual colours rather than sets, which will probably contain some colours that you never use. A white, black, red, blue, yellow, green and brown are all you need to begin with.

Coloured pencils are a very direct, easy-to-use drawing medium in their own right and they also work well in a mixed-media context – especially when combined with watercolour, inks or charcoal. For example, once dry, a watercolour sketch can be enhanced with lines and details added in pencil.

DRY COLOUR WORK

Traditional coloured pencils, which are also marketed as Artists' or Studio coloured pencils, are designed for dry colour work and they will suit all the conventional drawing techniques, whether you want to rely principally on line, or want to use overlaying and other effects. Try the following techniques:

▶ **Hatching** – *To suggest a light tone or broken coloured textural effect, apply a sequence of closely spaced hatched lines across the area. For a stronger tone and more intense colour, work*

*over the first set of lines with another sequence applied in the
opposite direction. Usually, hatched lines are drawn at an
angle of about 45 degrees. See also pages 66 and 67 and
Plates 4 and 5.*

▶ **Feathering** – *Use this method to create a transition of tone
from light to dark, or for blending one colour into another.
Work with short strokes of colour and, as you fill in an area,
either gradually alter the pressure or change to a lighter or
darker version of the colour. Alternatively, intersperse strokes
of one colour with strokes made with a different colour.*

▶ **Blending** – *For a more resolved and convincing blended effect,
work one colour over another and then slightly rub the surface
with a small piece of paper.*

▶ **Tonal variations** – *You can add interest and tonal variations
by altering the pressure on the pencil. For deep, rich tones
build up the colour effect with several layers.*

Other interesting techniques include using a putty eraser to soften
and blend colours; scratching out highlights with a sharp knife; and
using dots of different sizes, intensities and colours to add texture,
as in Plates 6, 7 and 8.

WATER-SOLUBLE PENCILS

Although they are similar in appearance to the traditional coloured
pencil, water-soluble pencils (also known as watercolour or aquarelle
pencils) offer more scope. You can make drawings that combine the
control and intensity of dry colour work with more subtle wash and
other 'watercolour' effects achieved by wetting coloured areas with
a brush and clean water. These pencils are also useful for adding
texture and detail to watercolour paintings.

In addition to working with washes and the various 'dry'
techniques described above for coloured pencils, you can draw on
damp paper to create a blurred, atmospheric quality or use a sharp
pencil to add detail over a wash area. Similarly, interesting results
are achieved by painting with colour picked up from the tip of a
pencil with a wet brush, or by wetting an area and then dabbing it

with tissue paper to create a soft, diffused effect. See Plates 9–13 for examples of different techniques.

PASTEL PENCILS

Pastel pencils are another excellent drawing medium that enables both control and versatility in approach. They are very useful for adding finishing touches, especially detail, to pastel paintings, but they also offer an interesting sketching medium in their own right. In contrast to pastel sticks, there is very little dust from pastel pencils, and essentially they are much easier to work with.

Insight

Pastel pencils work well on most types of paper, including coloured papers, drawing papers and watercolour papers – which will add texture. For drawings in which you want to combine pastel pencils with pastel sticks, choose a good quality paper, such as Canson Mi-Teintes.

Pastel pencils are more convenient to carry around and less likely to break than the soft pastel sticks, and this makes them a good choice for outdoor subjects.

With pastel pencils, you can lay in broad areas of colour, combining these with whatever definition and detail is required. And because they are made from pure pigment powder, these pencils are ideal for blending and creating quick atmospheric effects. Like true pastels, colours can be overlayed and rubbed together, and you can even wet them to give interesting wash, textural and surface qualities.

Pastels

Soft pastels are made from dry pigment mixed with a binder, such as gum arabic or gum tragacanth, and a preserver or extender. Round and square varieties are produced, both in the form of sticks about 5 cm long. The square pastels are firmer, making them suitable for detailed linear work as well as broad areas of colour. Pastel colour is opaque.

There is no mixing, thinning or particular preparation necessary with pastels, and consequently they encourage a direct, individual approach. The colours are dry and therefore instantly ready to work over, and they are permanent, with no risk of fading or sinking. Another advantage is the versatility of the medium: you can use a linear or mark-making technique or adopt a broader, almost painterly style. Pastels are excellent for carefully controlled studies made with line and blended tones, just as they are for a more spontaneous method of working, using freely applied marks and dabs of colour.

To maximize the range of possible techniques and effects, most artists use a combination of soft and hard pastels. Soft pastels will give the most sensitive marks and they produce the wonderful velvety bloom that is so characteristic of this medium. Hard pastels, which are normally made in square sticks, are firmer and thus, if required, can be sharpened to a point.

Most pastellists prefer to work on a rough-grained surface, as this allows a build-up of the medium for more textural results. However, smooth papers are also useful for certain subjects, especially portraits, linear work and sketching. If you haven't used pastels before and want to try them out, then you could start with an introductory set of, say, 12 colours. You can also buy individual sticks and thus gradually add to the initial selection with further colours that are appropriate for your subject matter and method of working. For landscape painting, for example, you would need a good choice of greens, blues and earth colours. See Plates 14 and 15.

PASTEL TECHNIQUES

You can work directly onto the pastel paper or card, or start with a watercolour or acrylic wash (or sequence of washes) to create an underpainting in which you can fix the basic composition, tonal values and mood for the drawing. An underpainting is particularly useful when working on textured white paper, because it will not only give a tonal value from which to build the relationship of lights and darks, but it also prevents flecks of white paper showing through the pastel and detracting from the impact of the finished drawing.

The general principal with pastel techniques – as indeed with most drawing techniques – is to start with the weak tones and lines and build up the thickness and intensity of the medium gradually. Mix colours either by alternating a stroke of one colour with that of another, and then blending the two together with a finger or small piece of cloth or paper, or by working one colour over another. Blow away unwanted dust and 'lift' mistakes with a kneadable or putty rubber.

Essentially, pastel drawings rely on developing colour, texture, depth and detail by working with a variety of strokes and so creating marks of different character and emphasis – similar, in fact, to the way you would use brushstrokes in a painting. You will need to develop a repertoire of strokes so that you can make an informed decision as to which type of mark will work best for a particular subject or effect.

The application of colour can vary from a pointillist technique (using small dots and dashes of colour made with the pastel stick held vertically) to broad, spontaneous strokes (made with the side of the pastel stick). Once the basic areas of colour and texture are in place, details can be added with the tip of a pastel stick that has been sharpened with a blade or sandpaper. But whatever techniques are used, the secret with pastel is not to overwork anything – to keep the marks and colours as lively and expressive as possible.

Insight

Unless they are protected in some way, finished pastel drawings will easily smudge if they are accidentally touched. Spray the finished drawing with fixative, or store it in a drawer, protecting the pastel surface with a sheet of tissue paper.

OIL PASTELS

Oil pastels will give a richer, waxier colour quality. These pastels are made by heating raw pigments with an oil-soluble wax binder to produce a buttery paste, which is then moulded into pastel sticks. As a result, oil pastels are water-resistant and, unlike soft pastels, they can be handled quite firmly without fear of breaking or creating dust. There are different shapes and sizes to choose from, in both round and square section lengths.

Oil pastels are a very straightforward, tactile medium to use, and as such they are ideal for bold, large-scale work involving vigorous, textural strokes and exploiting the power of colour. See Plate 17. Many different handling techniques are possible, including blending areas of colour with a brush or cotton bud dipped in white spirit, or exploiting sgraffito, resist or texture effects. The medium also offers a lot of exciting potential when used with inks, soft pastels, watercolour and other media.

Insight

Oil pastels won't smudge and therefore they are a good medium to use for sketchbook studies, especially when working outdoors.

Coloured inks

The choice of coloured inks includes calligraphy inks, drawing inks and acrylic inks, all of which suit pen and ink drawings, colour studies and mixed-media work. The main point to be aware of with inks is that many of the colours are quite intense, although more subtle tones are easily achieved by heavily diluting and/or intermixing colours. Note too that inks vary in their permanency and lightfast qualities and in whether they remain soluble or are water-resistant once dry. Try some experiments to check the particular qualities of your inks before using them for specific drawings.

The choice of drawing tools for use with coloured inks includes pens, brushes and airbrushes. You could try dip pens, with a variety of different nibs, mapping pens and, for more controlled work (depending on the type of ink), a reservoir pen or technical pen. Similarly, by experimenting with hog and soft hair brushes of different types and sizes, you can create a huge variety of sensitive and expressive effects. And additionally, of course, you can draw with coloured felt-tip, fibre-point and brush pens. See Plate 18.

The other key material is the paper. For linear work using a pen, the best surface is a smooth cartridge paper, a Hot-pressed watercolour paper, or Bristol board. However, for brush and wash techniques, or mixed-media work, you will need a thicker, more robust and absorbent surface, such as 140 lb (300 gsm) Not or Rough surface watercolour paper. Stretch the paper first, if you are going to use very diluted washes of colour. Refer to page 150 for advice on how to stretch paper.

INK TECHNIQUES

You can dilute water-based inks, such as Daler-Rowney Pearlescent Liquid Acrylic colours, with tap water, and shellac-based inks, such as Winsor & Newton Drawing Inks, with distilled water. If you mix shellac-based inks with tap water, the colours may separate slightly, although this can give an interesting effect in its own right. Melted ice from the inside of your freezer will provide a good source of distilled water!

....
Insight
Remember, you can exploit the different characteristics of water-soluble and water-resistant inks. For example, you can work on damp paper to create blurred marks and atmospheric effects, or re-wet areas made with water-soluble inks to modify them in some way.
....

Here are some other techniques:

▶ **Pen drawing** – *This is a useful technique for contour drawings and small line sketches and studies. Generally, the most successful results are achieved by restricting the colours to just two or three. Try combining lines and marks from different* nib widths or pens to add interest and convey specific effects in the drawing, as well as using hatching techniques and similar types of mark making to suggest form and tone.

▶ **Line and wash** – *You can work on smooth or slightly textured paper for this technique. Remember to stretch the paper if you intend using heavy washes of colour. A textured surface is ideal for a more expressive approach in which you want the lines to be less defined and the areas of colour more broken. As in Plate 20, you can either start with a line drawing made with a pen and then apply washes of appropriate colours to develop the idea further or, as in Plate 21, begin with the general areas of colour and work into these with a pen or pencil to add the necessary detail and definition. Test the colour washes on a piece of scrap paper before working on the actual drawing. If the colour is too strong, add more water to the wash.*

▶ **Brush drawings** – *Again, consider carefully which type of paper will best suit the subject matter and techniques you have in mind, as well as which brushes, inks and colour range to use. An extensive range of effects is possible by combining different types of inks, and intermixing colours, or exploiting the degree of opacity and translucency in different colours. You can work with strong colour direct from the bottle, a sequence of translucent glazes or opaque colours, or various tints made by mixing a selected colour with white. Another advantage with ink is that whites and highlights can be added at any stage in the work.*

▶ **Mixed media** – *Methods include using washes of ink as the underpainting for work in pastel; combining ink with areas, details, textures or other effects added in gouache, watercolour, oil pastel or coloured pencils; enriching parts of a watercolour painting with accents or passages worked in coloured inks; or using inks in conjunction with collage techniques. Additionally, there is a lot of scope for making abstract designs with ink and mixed media, or experimenting with resist techniques and textures which, as in watercolours, can be made by applying washes of colour over salt, oil pastel, masking fluid and so on. See Plates 23 and 24.*

Exercises

1   *Taking a subject of your choice, make a sequence of studies like those shown in Plate 1, working in colour with line and wash. You could try pencil with watercolour wash, or make a pen drawing with ink wash.*

2   *Look at the step-by-step coloured pencil drawings in Plates 6–8 and also Plate 9. Choose a beach scene of your own and make a well-resolved drawing in coloured or water-soluble coloured pencils.*

3   *Try a landscape drawing in soft pastels or oil pastels. See Plates 15 and 17.*

10 THINGS TO REMEMBER

1 Colour drawing skills are important, because colour is often the quality that most defines the mood and impact of the subject.

2 The range of colour media includes coloured pencils, pastels and inks. You can use these individually or combine them in mixed-media drawings.

3 To gain confidence with each colour medium, start with some experiments to see what effects are possible and how to vary the strength of colour.

4 A good technique to start with is to draw with line and colour. Make an outline drawing of your subject in pencil or pen and then add areas of colour in coloured pencils or by using weak watercolour or ink colour washes.

5 As well as working with a dry colour technique, you can also use water-soluble pencils and pastels to add subtle colour wash and texture effects to your drawing.

6 Initially, to assess the subject matter and help you understand the colour values, half-close your eyes and look for the main contrasts of strong and weak colours.

7 Try not to make assumptions about the colour of things. Observe and study the colour in the subject matter carefully.

8 Generally, drawings are more effective if the colour palette is restricted – perhaps to just five or six colours.

9 Check which type of paper will be best for the colour medium and effects you have in mind.

10 Drawing in colour will give you more scope to express your ideas successfully and in your own, individual way.

6

Observation and interpretation

In this chapter you will learn:
- *how to draw from direct observation*
- *how to focus on the most important qualities in the subject matter*
- *how to add feeling and personality to your drawings.*

Aims and objectives

Most artists prefer to work from actual, rather than imagined subject matter; they feel most confident making their drawings from direct observation. Of course, the advantage of this approach is that it offers a defined and constant source of reference for the drawing – you are able continually to relate what you have drawn to the subject matter in front of you and adjust the marks and effects as you think fit. The subject matter itself could be something you have deliberately chosen or arranged at home, or a landscape view or other scene that you have found outdoors.

Usually, you will want to create a drawing of the subject, and in this case realism and accuracy will be important considerations. On other occasions, you may decide to draw from the subject, which will allow you to be more selective and original in your approach. However, before starting any drawing you have to make various decisions. For instance, having chosen what to draw, you will need to consider how large the drawing is going to be, which medium and techniques will work best, and what sort of drawing you want. So, for each drawing, you will have certain aims and objectives. As the work progresses, you may, of course, decide to change your intentions, and at the end you can judge just how far you have succeeded in realizing the effects and impact you had in mind.

Insight

While you might have to slightly modify your objectives because of unforeseen problems or developments in the work, try not to deviate too far from the original intention for the drawing. Radical changes will impact on the whole drawing and they are usually very difficult to carry out successfully.

To begin with, it is wise to investigate different media, practise the basic techniques and do a lot of carefully observed drawings of a wide variety of subjects. Later, as your own style and ideas about drawing emerge, you will want to draw in a more subjective and personal way. But even those who draw from memory and imagination need the initial discipline of observation and the benefit of an accurate and extensive visual vocabulary of different shapes and subjects.

LOOKING AND UNDERSTANDING

Technical ability is very important, but it is of limited value on its own. As well, to create successful results, you will need skills in assessing and visualizing subject matter so that, from this process, you are able to convert what you see into elements and qualities that can be readily expressed through the means of drawing. Therefore, an essential part of learning to draw is learning how to look at and notice things. You cannot draw something accurately if you have not observed and studied it thoroughly enough. Successful representational drawings depend on a sound understanding of proportions, structure, form, detail, characteristics and so on, gained from careful observation.

Consequently, you can appreciate that even before you make any marks on the paper, drawing is already a matter of asking questions and reaching decisions. This is by far the best approach because, alternatively, if you only take a casual glance at something, it results in a very limited amount of information. So, try to get into the habit of looking at everything in a questioning way, which in turn will provide you with a greater degree of understanding and reference information for the subject matter. And equally, try to avoid general assumptions or preconceptions about the subject. Perhaps you have drawn it, or something like it, many times before. Nevertheless, examine the subject afresh; look for something new. In this way, you will keep your drawings lively and interesting.

FACTORS FOR SUCCESS

Drawing and observation go together, and therefore the best way to help yourself look at things carefully is to do as much drawing as possible. One way to encourage yourself to draw is to carry a sketchbook with you: there is more information on this in Chapter 7. You will soon discover that if you are really interested and excited by a subject, you are more likely to make a good drawing of it. Attitude and enthusiasm are other important factors that will influence your success. And, of course, you will need to practise and persevere. There will be good drawings and bad drawings, but quite often you will find that, even in your weakest drawings, there are some worthwhile qualities that help towards your general development.

> ### Insight
> Regular practice is the most useful. Draw as often as you can – if possible every day, even if this is only a small sketchbook study.

> ### Insight
> By all means be self-critical, for this will aid your progress. But don't take too much notice of those people who believe that a drawing is poor if it doesn't look virtually photographic. There is no single, correct way to draw!

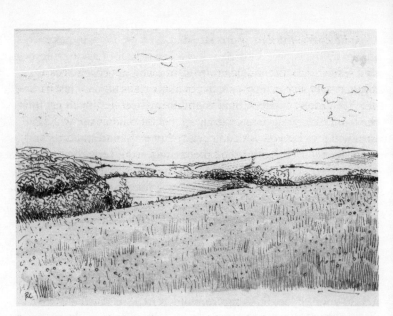

Illustration 6.1 Capturing the essence of a scene in sketch form, such as here, requires careful observation and quick decision-making. Ink and pencil.

You will notice that throughout this book there is an underlying emphasis on looking and understanding, and consequently straightforward observation drawings. This approach has been stressed because it will help you draw more confidently and successfully. However, in time, having gained a certain degree of confidence, you will probably find that you will want to draw with more freedom and self-expression.

As you learn more about drawing, you will discover that it is also concerned with expressing your feelings. From the same basis of observing and understanding the subject matter, you can interpret it in your own personal way, perhaps by emphasizing certain points or analyzing, selecting and developing particular aspects. Now let's look at these various approaches in more detail. Bear in mind that sometimes, to successfully achieve the effects and impact you have in mind for the drawing, you may have to involve more than one approach.

OBSERVATION

While both drawing and painting might each be considered as a distinct discipline in its own right, in many ways they are inseparable, for it is difficult to define rigid boundaries. Creating a painting often involves a lot of preliminary drawing, just as making a drawing sometimes includes brush and paint techniques. In the past, drawings were mainly regarded as useful preparatory work for a painting rather than as separate works of art. Most drawings were made as studies, for information and research, or as composition roughs and cartoons.

Although the scope and importance of drawing has developed, its original role remains vital. Whether they are employed in preparatory work, in exploring different ideas and concepts, or in collecting information, drawing skills are essential to all artists, designers and craftspeople. For many, there is still a need to make carefully observed drawings from life.

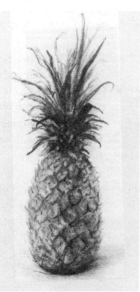

Illustration 6.2 This is an example of a careful drawing made from direct observation, with the intention of capturing an accurate likeness of the subject. Charcoal and charcoal pencil.

When we set out to make an accurate likeness of an object or scene before us, this is known as working from direct observation. In such drawings, we are working objectively, aiming for a true representation without any elaboration, emphasis or selectivity. We need to be inquisitive; the importance of looking, noticing and understanding has already been stressed.

Before you start some observation drawings of your own, think about these points:

▶ *the selection and arrangement of the different shapes or objects involved and how these can be used to make an interesting composition*
▶ *the relative size and position of individual shapes and their structure: how are the shapes formed?*
▶ *light and dark values: tonal quality*
▶ *colour, surface textures and details*
▶ *the sort of effects you want and therefore the most suitable drawing medium (or media) and type of paper.*

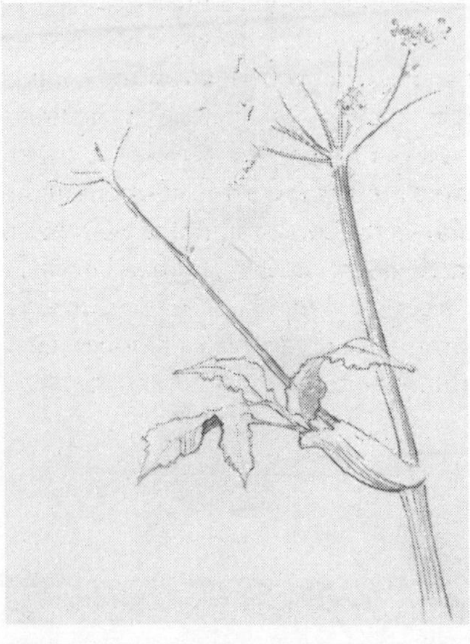

Illustration 6.3 Observation study. Stage 1: Considering the basic structure of the subject.

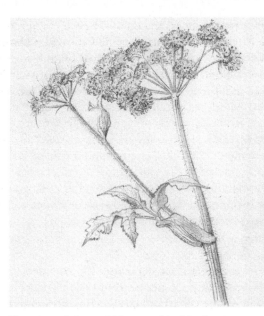

Illustration 6.4 Observation study. Stage 2: Adding tone and detail. Pencil.

Consider these points in relation to Illustrations 6.3 and 6.4.
Getting a good structure for the drawing is important. If the
basic shapes are sound, this will give you the confidence to
develop the work in the way that you wish. The first step in any
drawing is to plan it out roughly so as to fit the paper and such
that the main shapes are in the correct positions and proportions.
Illustration 6.3 shows the sort of initial sketch that helps in
plotting the main elements, which can then be worked over in
more detail and accuracy. Note how in the completed pencil
drawing, in Illustration 6.4, various techniques have been used
to show different tonal effects, textures and surface details.

Analysis

Observation may, of course, include a certain amount of analysis,
although it is usually concerned with making a single drawing from
a single viewpoint. Sometimes we need more than this and want

to examine the subject in greater detail. In such cases, a whole series of drawings might be necessary. These could show different viewpoints as well as consider all the factors listed for observation drawings. Alternatively, several drawings could be made from the same viewpoint, but with each drawing focusing on a different aspect: form, colour, texture, detail and so on. Such an approach will probably require a variety of media and techniques.

Therefore, demanding detailed enquiry and involving a range of drawing skills, analytical drawings entail sound practice for the beginner – indeed, for any artist. Occasionally, it is a good idea to really probe a subject in this way, and such drawings will provide valuable preparatory information and reference for more elaborate or imaginative works.

Natural forms make ideal subject matter for analytical drawings. They can be twisted and examined from various angles and often have interesting colours, details and textures to deal with. Sometimes, like the fish studies in Illustration 6.5, they can be cut open and drawn in sectional view as well. With more complex subjects, another possibility is to make a line drawing of the complete shape and then isolate a section for particular analysis.

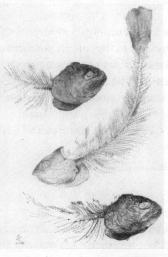

Illustration 6.5 Where a subject offers a number of interesting qualities, try making several drawings, focusing on a different quality in each one. Pencil, charcoal and ink wash.

Selection

Observation and analysis are objective approaches that lead to informative, representational drawings. While these processes might form the basis of most of your work, they are not always an end in themselves. As you gain in confidence and skill, you may wish to introduce a more personal way of interpreting the subjects that interest you.

None of us sees a subject in quite the same way, even when we are attempting a drawing from direct observation. Our choice of size, viewpoint, medium and technique gives the work a degree of individuality, even here. But we can go further than this: we can select and emphasize those features and characteristics within the subject matter that appeal to us most. Often, we are inspired by a subject for a particular reason. We may be struck by its dramatic qualities of light and dark, for example, or its interesting shape and form. These will be the features to stress in our drawing. Thus, we are in fact interpreting what we see, conveying by a process of selection those qualities which, in our opinion, create the essence of the subject.

Insight

To help with the decision-making regarding the most important qualities to capture in your drawing, you may find it useful to start with a sequence of small 'thumbnail' sketches. These will help concentrate your thoughts and prevent you from including unnecessary detail.

INTERPRETATION AND TECHNIQUE

All drawings must involve selection to a degree. There has to be some simplification and selection, even in the most objective approach. However skilful the artist, no one is capable of capturing a perfect likeness of the subject matter or of accurately representing every detail and feature. And, of course, the drawing materials and processes themselves limit the degree of realism that can be achieved. On the other hand, although we might want to draw in a more individual and expressive way, equally this will usually benefit from careful observation and from deciding which qualities are important about the subject.

Inextricably linked with interpretation is the artist's choice of medium and technique. With an idea involving atmospheric and diffused colour effects, for example, soft pastels would be much more suitable than coloured pencils, which might give a more linear effect. Look at the charcoal drawing in Illustration 6.6. Here, the choice of medium has enabled a successful impression of form and space and an interesting composition and interplay of different shapes.

> **Insight**
> Sometimes, during a drawing, you will think of alternative, perhaps better ways of interpreting the subject – maybe by using a different medium or technique. Save these ideas for separate drawings.

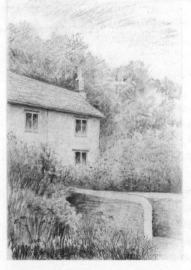

Illustration 6.6 The choice of medium and technique is always important in the successful interpretation of a subject. Charcoal and charcoal pencil.

Feeling

Drawings can also show mood and emotion and be created in a much more spontaneous, subjective and expressive way. The vigorous drawings of Van Gogh, for example, are charged with great passion and feeling.

It takes time to develop the ability to draw with this sort of freedom and sensitivity: it usually evolves only after a great deal of practice and experience. You need to be accomplished in, and confident with, different techniques, and allow the drawing to be governed principally by your emotional response to the subject matter – as opposed to the dispassionate approach of an objective drawing. To draw with feeling, you must be really excited and inspired by an idea; it must be something that you really want to draw.

Lively drawings of this type seem to imply a quick method of working and a sort of outpouring of inspiration. This is largely true. However, obviously not every subject will provoke a passionate response. In many of your drawings, you will be looking for a more straightforward approach. But there will be times when you are inspired to make this sort of drawing and will want to experiment with a looser technique.

EXPERIMENT!

Medium, subject matter and individual artistic style each play a part in creating drawings with feeling. Any medium can be used sensitively and expressively, but you may find some media, like pastel and charcoal, less inhibiting than others. Be prepared to experiment occasionally. Similarly, try a variety of subjects and ideas. A derelict industrial landscape, for instance, can be just as inspiring as a moonlit lake. And don't worry about finding a style – this will come in time. Your style will be influenced by a wide range of things, perhaps including your study of other artists' work or the particular medium and methods you most often use.

Sketching techniques are a great help in developing quick and spontaneous ways of drawing. Chapter 7 deals with these in more detail. Look at the landscape drawing shown in Illustration 6.7. The aim here was to focus on capturing the mood and feeling of the scene, rather than any detailed description.

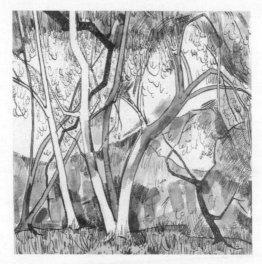

Illustration 6.7 A focus on mood and feeling will often lead to a more expressive approach to drawing, as here. Pen and ink.

Developing

Sometimes, the subject before you acts as a sort of starting point or trigger for a more stylized, imaginative or even abstract approach. It provides you with the basis of an idea that you can develop or interpret in an extremely individual way. You might emphasize or exaggerate, distort or simplify. You could decide to use an unusual viewpoint or work in a limited colour or tonal range. There are many possibilities.

Such drawings often result from an intellectual process – that is, by applying some kind of theory or restriction to the way that the work is developed. For example, if you look at the drawing in

Illustration 6.8, you will see that I have simplified the shapes to create a strong composition, and then have concentrated on using mainly a hatching technique to develop the tonal effects. In other words, I have set distinct aims and limits for the drawing.

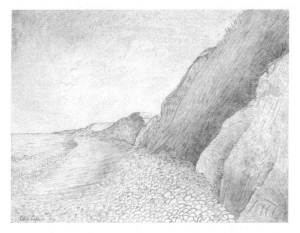

Illustration 6.8 Set clear aims for your drawings. Here, I have concentrated on contrasts of tone and texture. Pencil.

Exercises

1 *Work from a flowering pot plant. Draw from direct observation, making two drawings, each from a different viewpoint. If it is a complex or large plant, select two different parts of it. Aim for carefully observed drawings that you could send to someone else to show them exactly what the plant looks like.*

2 *Now try a contrasting approach. Make a third drawing with a stick of charcoal or pastel, working freely and vigorously, aiming to express the general characteristics of the plant or focusing on the qualities that you find particularly interesting. Make this drawing larger than life size; work on an A3 size sheet of paper or larger.*

10 THINGS TO REMEMBER

1 *Whatever you are drawing, start by deciding on your aims and objectives for the work: what exactly do you want to include in your drawing, and how do you want to express it?*

2 *The features that most impress you about a subject are the ones to most stress in the drawing.*

3 *Key decisions must also include how large to make your drawing and which medium (or media) to use.*

4 *All drawings must involve selection and simplification to some degree.*

5 *Sometimes, particularly when you are working on the spot and want sketches as reference material from which to make a larger drawing later, it is a good idea to make a sequence of drawings, each covering a different aspect of the subject matter.*

6 *Remember that drawings can be subjective as well as objective: they can show mood and emotion and be created in a much more spontaneous, expressive way.*

7 *Also, if you wish, you can draw from memory and imagination.*

8 *Learning to look at and understand what you see is just as important as learning drawing skills.*

9 *A willingness to experiment and try new ideas will be an important factor in helping you develop different drawing skills.*

10 *Your drawing style is something that will develop gradually, perhaps influenced by your study of other artists' work or the particular media and methods you most often use.*

7

....

Keeping a sketchbook

In this chapter you will learn:
- *why it is important to keep a sketchbook*
- *how to choose a sketchbook*
- *which techniques to use in your sketchbook.*

_____

An invaluable resource

A sketchbook is a vital item of equipment that will suit a variety of purposes. In your sketchbook, you can 'think' with your pencil, solve problems and store useful information. Generally speaking, it is not the place for highly finished drawings, although occasionally you may wish to include a more resolved study, if time, conditions and inclination seem to favour it.

Try to use your sketchbook every day, even if this is only for a few minutes. This will help you practise and develop your drawing skills. Additionally, your sketchbook will come in handy for research, ideas, thoughts, jottings, experiments, problem solving, notes, planning, roughs and so on. And as always, don't be afraid to try out fresh ideas and use different media and methods in your sketchbook. You will see from this section just how valid sketching is and what a variety of techniques you can use.

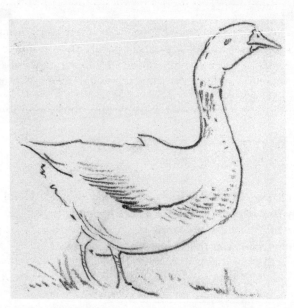

Illustration 7.1 As here, although quite simple, a sketch can be very informative. Charcoal pencil.

CHOOSING A SKETCHBOOK

Sketchbooks are sold under a variety of names, including sketch blocks, drawing pads, layout pads, and drawing books. A good choice to begin with is an A4 spiral-bound cartridge paper sketchbook for general use plus a small, pocket-size one to jot down ideas, notes and flashes of inspiration as they occur. Cartridge paper is fine for most media and techniques but, as your work progresses, you may find that you need a particular type and size of sketchbook which better suits a certain medium and way of working. For example, if you work mostly in pen and ink, you will find that the smooth paper in a layout pad is best. You can also buy sketchbooks consisting of sheets of watercolour paper (for brush and wash ideas) and coloured pastel paper (for chalks, pastels, charcoal and similar soft drawing media techniques). Remember that the type of paper will influence how the medium responds, so think carefully about the kind of sketchbook that will suit you best.

Insight

You might like to try making your own sketchbook using an A4 ring binder and loose sheets of paper. The advantage with this is that you can combine sheets of different types of paper and therefore increase the scope to use different media and techniques.

Ideas and experiments

Think of your sketchbook as your personal visual notebook. You don't have to show it to anyone else, and therefore you can work freely, without inhibition. Generally, a sketchbook isn't the place for highly finished work; on the contrary, it could include lots of drawings that are only partially successful. In fact, this is one of its main functions – as a place where you can try out ideas and solve problems, so that you avoid mistakes elsewhere.

Insight

Don't tear out pages from your sketchbook. If a drawing is unsuccessful, make a new sketch on the next page, showing how you learned from the mistakes in the first attempt. By keeping everything in your sketchbook you can more readily appreciate the progress you have made. Also, even a poor sketch will usually have some qualities that are useful and worth preserving.

If you are planning a holiday, visiting somewhere, having a day out in the country, or going anywhere that looks potentially promising from a drawing or ideas point of view, then remember to take your sketching things! You never know when you will come across an interesting subject to draw; you will often find ideas in the most unlikely places. So, jot them down in your sketchbook, and in this way build up a collection of reference and outline ideas that you can develop later. For your own interest, and to help jog your memory about the subject when you look at the sketch later, include a note of the place and the date of your drawing.

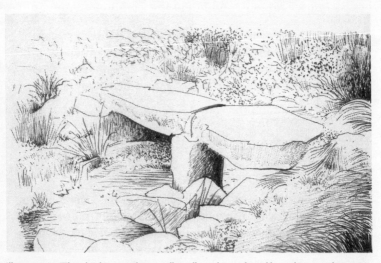

Illustration 7.2 When sketching outside, you will usually need to work quickly, so choose a technique you are confident with. Pen and ink.

As well as trying out new media and techniques in your sketchbook, also use it as a way of familiarizing yourself with a subject before you start on a more resolved study. Learn to introduce yourself to subjects and ideas by this means, as in the drawings in Illustrations 7.2 and 7.3. Quick drawings similar to these will help you assess a subject and its likely problems, getting you looking and thinking. Notice also the different techniques used here: a mapping pen in Illustration 7.2 and charcoal in Illustration 7.3. Charcoal is an ideal medium for quick results, and the line techniques discussed in Chapter 3 are also useful for sketching. And equally, of course, sketches can work as effective, interesting drawings in their own right.

Insight

Many artists find 'portrait' sketchbooks easier to hold and work in than 'landscape' ones. When they want to draw a wide view or tackle something on a larger scale or in more detail, they work across a double page.

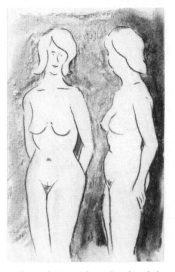

Illustration 7.3 Sketches are a good way of getting to know the subject before you start on a more detailed drawing. Charcoal.

Drawing and research

Quite often you will need more than the bones of an idea – you will need good reference material from which to work. In this case, your sketchbook might be used for making careful studies, researching form and movement, exploring different viewpoints, or looking more specifically at texture, structure, details and colour reference. Sometimes you will find that a sequence of sketches is necessary to help you develop the final study, while on other occasions the sort of analysis shown in Illustration 7.4 will lead to a better understanding of the structure and form of the subject matter and thus give you greater confidence when working on a more detailed drawing.

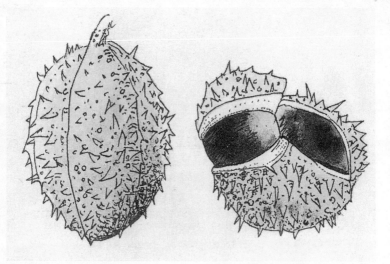

Illustration 7.4 Sometimes in your sketches you may want to explore different aspects of the same subject. Pen and wash.

Your sketchbook will be more interesting and useful if you try out different media rather than only use pencil. Pastel is good for quick colour studies, charcoal excellent for broad tonal work, and there is a variety of free-flowing fast-drying pens to choose from for line techniques. Additionally, you can combine work in pen and pencil with quick brush and wash effects, either in tone with diluted Indian ink, or in colour with watercolour or thinned coloured drawing inks. Water-soluble pencils are ideal for any colour sketches in which you need to incorporate line and solid colour or wash effects.

Insight

You may need to reacquaint yourself with some of the different media and techniques that can be used. If so, look again at Chapters 2 and 5.

SKETCHING TRIPS

Obviously, most sketching is done out-of-doors, concentrating on subjects such as landscapes, buildings, street scenes, harbours and so on. Here is a reminder of what you might need for sketching trips:

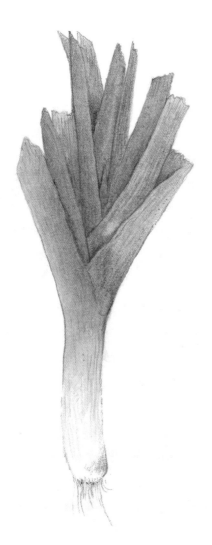

Plate 13 Leek study. Stage 3: Drawing over the blended colours to intensify the tonal qualities where necessary and add some detail. *Water-soluble coloured pencils.*

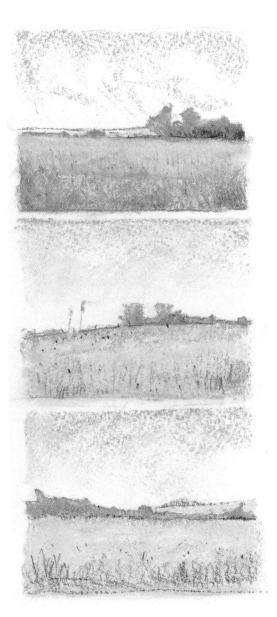

Plate 14 Try pastel for making quick colour 'notes' –
simple location sketches like these. If you wet the
pastel with a brush and some clean water, as I have
done in the top sketch, this enhances the colour and
gives a watercolour effect.

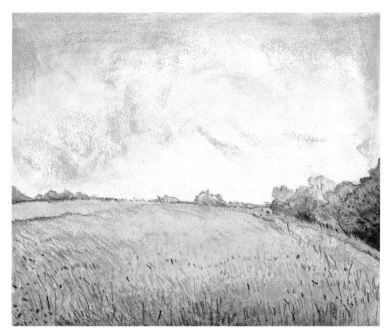

Plate 15 Landscape sketch. *Pastel*.

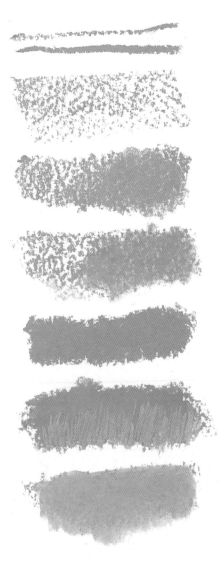

Plate 16 These experiments with oil pastel show lines, broken tone, overlaid colours, solid colour, scratching into colour, and creating a blended effect by wiping the colour with a small piece of cloth dipped into a little turpentine.

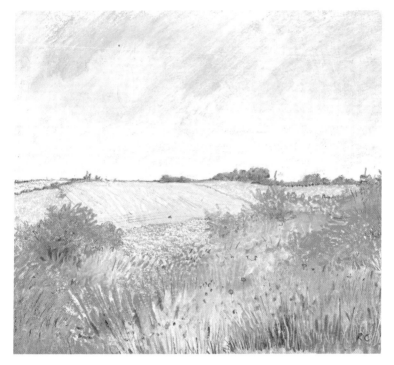

Plate 17 Oil pastels are an excellent medium for location sketches because they do not smudge and they can be used in a very direct way.

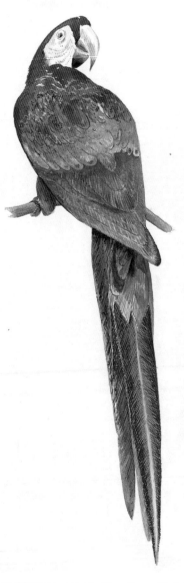

Plate 18 Water-soluble fibre-tip and felt-tip pens work very well over watercolour washes, and lines and marks can be softened by wetting them with a brush dipped in clean water. Allow the initial washes to dry before drawing over them with the pens.

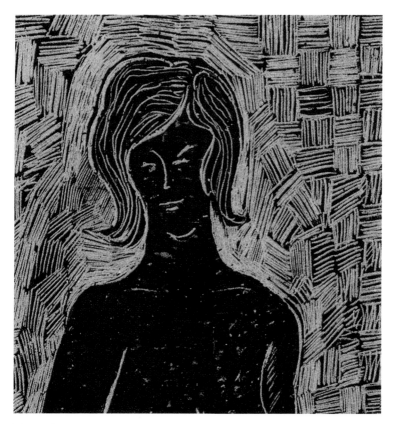

Plate 19 This sgraffito drawing was made by first shading a sheet of paper with orange wax crayon, then applying a wash of Indian ink over this. When the ink was dry, I 'drew' with the tip of a needle – scratching through the surface to reveal the colour beneath.

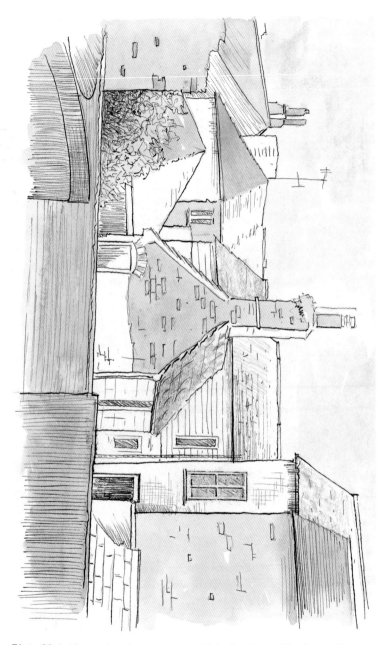

Plate 20 Adding colour to your pen and ink drawings will enhance the result. *Mapping pen, Indian ink and watercolour washes.*

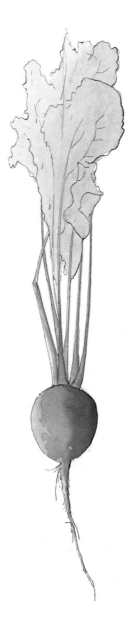

Plate 21 A simple pen and wash study. *Mapping pen, Indian ink and watercolour washes.*

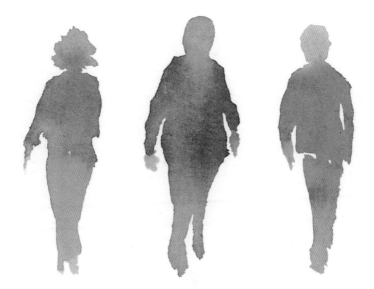

Plate 22 Try some figure sketches like these, using a brush and wash technique.

Plate 23 Sometimes, a good way to interpret a subject is to use a combination of different media. Wash, wax crayon, pastel and coloured pencil techniques have all been used in this drawing.

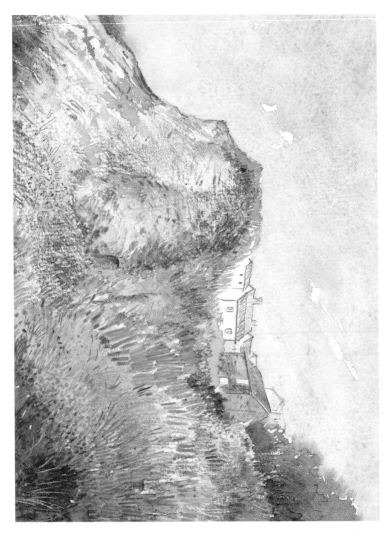

Plate 24 Again here, I felt the subject would benefit from a mixed-media approach. *Graphite, coloured and water-soluble coloured pencils, with wax crayon and watercolour, on watercolour paper.*

- a sketchpad or a small drawing board and some sheets of paper
- pencils, pens, charcoal, pastels and other colour media such as water-soluble pencils
- a small, screwtop bottle of water, brushes, cloth, craft knife, eraser, bulldog clips to hold down paper, fixative
- a folding stool or something to sit on
- a rucksack or something to carry everything in
- suitable clothing, food and drink.

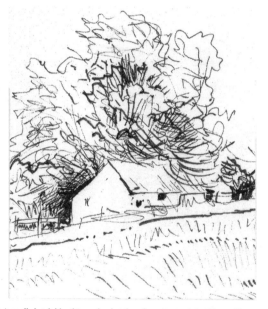

Illustration 7.5 A small sketch like this need only take a few minutes, but will provide a permanent reminder of the scene. Pen and ink.

PRACTICAL CONSIDERATIONS

Be adaptable and prepared for changes in the weather; if you are unable to find or draw exactly what you intended, then try something else. For example, if the challenging landscape view that you hoped to draw is obliterated by a sudden rainstorm, then perhaps you can find a sheltered spot from which to make some individual studies of clouds, trees or other aspects of the landscape.

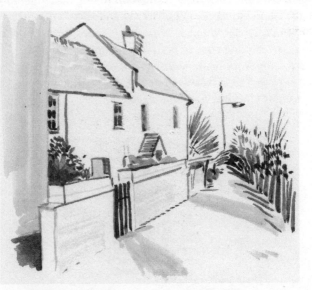

Illustration 7.6 Another useful sketching method is to draw with a brush and then add one or two tonal washes. Brush and diluted Indian ink.

Similarly, there has to be some give and take when sketching animals, which naturally cannot be expected to stand still for very long. Here, you may have to work on several sketches at once. If an animal moves after you have started sketching, then the best plan is to begin another drawing, based on the new position. You can add some more to the original sketch if the animal resumes the pose you began with.

You will normally have to work quite fast when sketching outside, so to save time, ignore those aspects of the subject which you can easily remember or which you can jot down in note form. Stick to an approach that focuses on the essential information about the main shapes and characteristics of the subject. Think of the sort of angle or viewpoint you want, and choose a sketching technique that suits the effect you are after and allows you to work quickly.

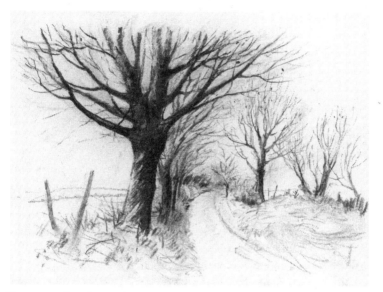

Illustration 7.7 Charcoal is a wonderful medium for quick, spontaneous sketches. This sketch was made with a single stick of charcoal, holding it at various angles to create marks of different thickness and intensity.

Notes and photographs

You can supplement any sketches, research studies, experiments and details with written notes. Sometimes there just isn't enough time to jot down everything you need to know in the form of drawing, or you may, for example, be restricted to black and white when you need some colour reference. If so, do as I have done in Illustration 7.8 – add a few words to your drawing to remind you of things.

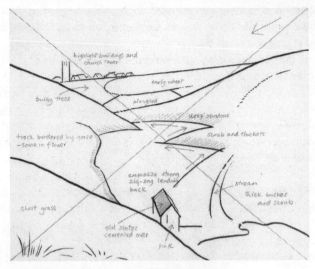

Illustration 7.8 Brief location sketch with added notes. Fibre-pen and pencil.

Photographs provide another form of reference. Again, you may run out of time, need something in colour, want some reference about a particular detail, or would benefit from a range of viewpoints and different composition suggestions. But look on photographs as an aid to your drawing rather than something to be slavishly copied, and whenever you use them, try to ensure that they are your own. If you were the photographer, it means that you have experienced the actual scene or subject matter and consequently you will be able to support the information provided by the photographs with your own recollections and feelings about what you saw.

You can use photographs for:

▶ **additional reference** – *either as a general reminder of a subject, or for a piece of specific information which you could use in part of a resolved drawing later on*
▶ **starting points** – *as the basis of an idea to develop or interpret in your own way in the form of sketches or drawings*
▶ **fleeting moments** – *for action subjects such as a speeding car or someone diving into a swimming pool (you simply would not have time to sketch these subjects effectively)*

▶ **composition aids** – *to provide you with a number of different viewpoints and suggestions for composition alternatives.*

One of the reasons why you should not copy photographs is that they tend to distort distance, perspective and colour, and so they cannot be relied upon to be completely truthful. But equally important is the fact that, no matter how technically sound the final image, simply reworking an idea from a photograph will probably result in a dull drawing, for it is likely to lack spontaneity and discovery.

Indeed, part of the fun and satisfaction of drawing is that, during the working process, there are usually some surprises – ideas and effects materialize which you hadn't expected. Consequently, the nature of the finished drawing depends partly on how these discoveries are dealt with – whether you accept and exploit them, or whether they are rejected. The danger with photographs is that they offer all the answers before you start work; there is nothing left to find out. And obviously this could stifle any sense of originality, energy and feeling in the drawing.

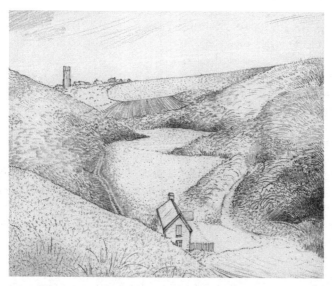

Illustration 7.9 Studio drawing made from the sketch in Illustration 7.8. Pencil.

Exercise

1   Choose an outdoor theme that appeals to you, such as
    buildings of local interest, tree forms, animals, people
    shopping, shadows and reflections, and so on. Over
    a period of time, make a series of reference drawings
    in your sketchbook that will help you compose a
    well-finished, studio-based drawing later on. Try
    different media and techniques, including some work
    in colour.
2   Make a sequence of sketches on the theme of water.
3   When you are next out for the day in the country,
    try making one or two general landscape sketches.
    See Illustrations 7.2, 7.5, 7.7 and 7.9.

10 THINGS TO REMEMBER

1 *Sketching will help you develop your drawing skills. Try to use your sketchbook every day.*

2 *Your sketchbook is your own personal visual notebook – you don't have to show it to anyone else, so feel free to use it without inhibition.*

3 *Draw any subjects that appeal to you and also use your sketchbook for testing out ideas and experimenting with different media and techniques.*

4 *As well as your main sketchbook, buy yourself a small pocket-size one that you can carry around with you and use for jotting down interesting ideas wherever you find them.*

5 *Keep to the essentials in a sketch – there won't be time to work in detail. Add some written notes if this helps.*

6 *Sometimes you may need to make a series of sketches in order to collect sufficient information from which to develop a more resolved studio drawing or painting later.*

7 *For colour sketches, try water-soluble colour pencils.*

8 *Pastel and charcoal are excellent media for quick sketches, but they are likely to smudge, so don't forget to spray them with fixative.*

9 *Take some photographs as additional reference, but try not to rely on photographs alone.*

10 *You can carry everything you need for sketching in a small rucksack. Look at the list on page 109.*

8

Design principles

In this chapter you will learn:
- *how to make a good design*
- *how to use perspective*
- *how to understand scale and proportion.*

What is design?

Whatever the appeal of a subject, to succeed as a drawing it must somehow involve an interpretation that is founded on a strong and visually pleasing design or composition. For, as well as providing the 'scaffolding' to help build and develop a drawing, the design plays a vital part in creating interest and impact. Indeed, it is often the key factor in producing an eye-catching and original result.

Design refers to the way that you arrange, balance and contrast the different shapes and other aspects that you wish to include in your drawing. It is obviously concerned with the subject matter and how this is presented within the picture area, but equally it must involve a consideration of the basic drawing elements such as line, mass, tone and colour. The choice of viewpoint or angle from which to draw the subject matter is always an important influence on the design, of course, as is how you contrast bold, general areas with smaller, detailed ones and so on. So, as you draw, you have to bear in mind that the distribution of tones or colours, the media and techniques being used, details and textures, and what you wish to emphasize and focus attention on, are all interrelated to the overall design or composition.

Even when you are drawing just a single object, it is essential to consider its size and position against the background area. For design relates to the whole sheet of paper, and therefore in the design process you need to think carefully about the relative importance of the positive elements (the main shapes of the subject matter) and the negative areas (the background shapes and spaces).

HOW TO MAKE A GOOD DESIGN

Generally, the most successful designs are those in which the shapes are arranged in such a way that your eye is led around the drawing, your attention is kept within the picture area, and you focus on a particular point of interest. The more drawings you make, the more you will find that good design often depends just as much on what you decide to leave out as on the way you organize and emphasize the remaining shapes.

Here again, there is no magic formula for success. As with other aspects of drawing, with design the best approach is to carefully study the theory, advice and various considerations that apply and, while you are drawing, take these into account as much as you feel is necessary. But don't be too influenced by 'rules'. Remember that your drawings should reflect something about you, rather than conform to a certain process. So, by all means draw with an awareness of accepted design principles, for this is sure to help. But also be guarded by your own instinct and ideas.

Drawing requires constant thought: with design you need to be fully aware of elements such as rhythm, balance, harmony and contrast, and in consequence you should always be able to justify the decisions you make about particular combinations and arrangements. One way of helping your deliberations about design is to study the work of other artists. Have a look at some drawings by well-known artists. Consider the way they have designed each work, how they have made their drawings interesting and exciting, whether they have used a focal point or created part of each drawing that particularly attracts your attention, and so on. Try asking the same questions about your own drawings – this should encourage you to think about design in a more confident way.

COMPOSITION SKETCHES

Your initial thoughts about the design for a drawing won't necessarily offer the strongest and most interesting idea to work from, of course. Particularly in the case of large, studio drawings, it is essential that the design is carefully considered before making a start. Once the drawing is in progress, it can be quite difficult to make changes to aspects of design that appear to be weak.

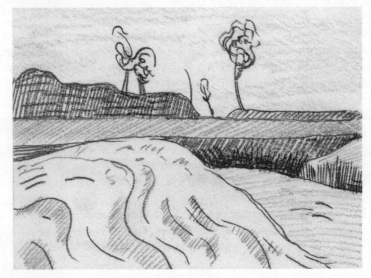

Illustration 8.1 Composition sketch 1. Pencil and charcoal pencil.

A good way to explore different design alternatives is to make a series of quick, simple sketches, like those in Illustrations 8.1 and 8.2. In the first Illustration, the distribution of the main shapes, especially the horizontal lines through the middle and the position of the trees, gives a rather balanced effect. In Illustration 8.2 on

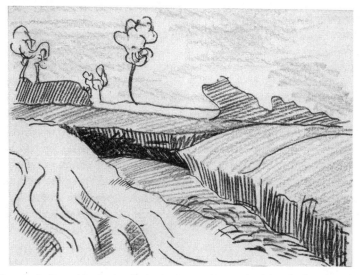

Illustration 8.2 Composition sketch 2. Altering the viewpoint to create a less balanced and consequently more interesting composition. Pencil and charcoal pencil.

the other hand, the trees are confined to the left-hand side and the viewpoint has been altered somewhat so as to create a more flowing and imbalanced design. Use non-fussy media like charcoal or pastel for roughs of this sort. For easy comparison, they can be done as a sequence on a large sheet of paper, or you can do them in your sketchbook.

Insight

Keep your composition sketches quick and simple. They needn't be very large and they only need to show the main shapes.

BASIC DIVISIONS

In dividing up the picture area into various shapes and spaces, we are essentially concerned with proportions. Generally speaking, a drawing that uses identical, balanced or totally symmetrical proportions in its basic composition will have far less overall impact than one that does not. But, like any 'rule' in drawing, it is true that this one is often broken, and indeed very effectively, by many accomplished artists. Nevertheless. it is usually best to avoid compositions that use equal divisions of the drawing area, either vertically or horizontally. For example, this would apply to a landscape in which the horizon was placed exactly halfway up the paper.

Instead, you could try designs that exploit a diagonal or triangular division of the picture area, or consider a division based on thirds – a design principle that artists have used since Renaissance times. Based on the Golden Section (or Golden Mean), a proportion that is found in nature and that is generally accepted to create an aesthetically pleasing arrangement, the 'thirds' principle can be applied equally effectively to figurative or abstract drawings.

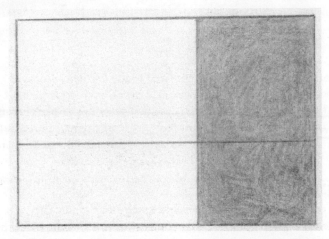

Illustration 8.3 Dividing a sheet of paper based on the Golden Section principle, in the ratio of 2:3.

The approximate ratio or proportions in the Golden Section is 5:8, but most artists like to simplify this even further and think in terms of thirds. Thus, a key feature of the composition (essentially the focal point) is placed about one-third (or two-thirds) of the distance across the painting – either horizontally or vertically. Although this is a composition technique based on theory, nevertheless it is one that always seems to work well.

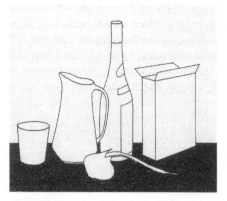

Illustration 8.4 Composition sketch. Notice that the grouping is rather equally spaced and balanced.

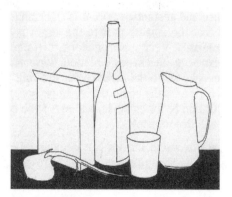

Illustration 8.5 Composition sketch. This is a better arrangement with more interesting spaces, although still rather symmetrical in the overall design.

Some other useful points about composition are demonstrated in Illustrations 8.4–8.6. In Illustration 8.4, you will notice that the objects are in a straight row and that they are spaced fairly evenly apart. Additionally, the horizon line is straight across and, with the bottle in the middle, the general arrangement is quite symmetrical. These are all potentially negative points: things that do not contribute to the excitement or impact of the design. In Illustration 8.5, some improvements have been made: the objects are not so spread out, but although the arrangement is more interesting, the bottle is still very central and the bases of the objects remain level.

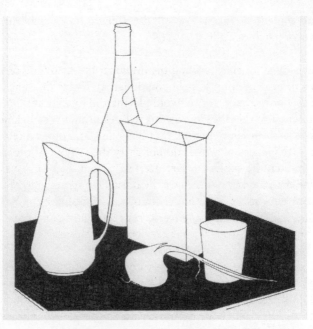

Illustration 8.6 Composition sketch. Here there is more movement in the design and the grouping is generally more exciting. Fibre-pen.

Now look at the composition in Illustration 8.6. Isn't this much better? There is greater movement and direction, more interesting spaces, and the general composition is now not so rigid and balanced. These are the sort of points to think about, not only when arranging a still life group, but regarding the selection and composition of any idea.

FOCAL POINT

Drawings need some drama in the way that the composition is devised; if there is equal interest and emphasis throughout the drawing, it is not likely to be very exciting. One method for creating a sense of drama is to contrast large, broadly expressed areas with the detail of a focal point, at the same time ensuring that the eye is led to the focal point in an interesting way. For example, in a landscape or townscape subject, the focal point could be a figure, while in an interior or still life it might be a particular object or even a patch of light.

In devising a 'journey' around the drawing, there are one or two points to bear in mind to help you design an image that has more impact. For instance, try to avoid placing the focal point in the central area of the drawing, as this will result in a very balanced design effect. Similarly, check that diagonals and other directional lines or sequences of shapes do not carry the eye out of the picture area. In fact, the subject matter itself will often suggest ways of leading the viewer's eye around the drawing and arriving at a focal point. A good composition will contribute to holding the viewer's attention and thus encouraging them to look more and more at the drawing, thereby discovering new depths and qualities.

With experience, you will discover how to experiment with the relative weight and position of different shapes and how these must correlate with tone, colour, texture, line and other qualities. Composition is all about balancing one thing against another and you will soon find that there are plenty of exciting ways of creating order in a drawing, yet at the same time directing the eye on an interesting journey around it. So don't be afraid to try different arrangements or to take a chance with the composition. And, although it is always a good idea to plan the main elements of the composition so that you have a framework to build on, undoubtedly the drawing will be livelier and fresher if there is something about the composition that is discovered and developed during the working process.

USING A VIEWFINDER

Some subjects are complicated and extensive, and you may find that it is very difficult to know which part to concentrate on for your drawing. Busy street scenes, panoramic landscapes, and general views fall into this category; there may be many different potentially good ideas to choose from. The viewpoint and scope of the view are always vital considerations in achieving a good composition.

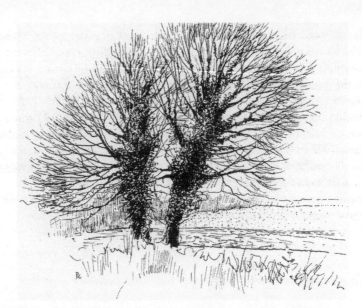

Illustration 8.7 As here, it is possible to use a more centrally placed feature in the composition, providing the shapes either side of it detract from, rather than reinforce the sense of balance. Pen and ink.

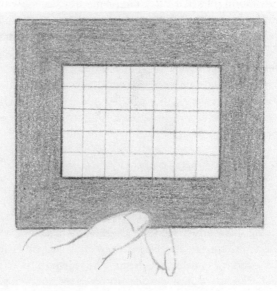

Illustration 8.8 A simple card viewfinder.

To help you isolate parts of a complex subject in order to determine which area will make the best drawing, you could use a cardboard viewfinder. Make this by cutting an aperture of about 2 cm × 3.5 cm in the middle of a sheet of 10 cm × 13.5 cm thin card, or make a slightly larger version if you intend drawing on a big scale. You could leave the middle section open or, as in Illustration 8.8, glue a piece of clear Perspex across it, with grid lines drawn on it, or make the grid lines by gluing lengths of cotton to the back. The squares on the grid will help you estimate where one shape comes in relation to another. With one eye closed, look through the viewfinder and move it around to compare different composition ideas. Try it both ways round – landscape (horizontally) and portrait (vertically).

Cropping

The composition and the impact of a finished drawing can sometimes be improved by cropping – in other words reducing the size of the drawing. Use two 'L' shaped pieces of card like those shown in Illustration 8.9. These can be moved around on the drawing to 'frame' the best section. The drawing is then trimmed to the desired size.

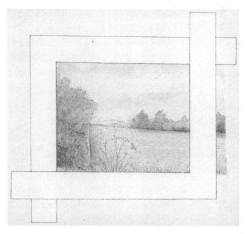

Illustration 8.9 Using two right angles of card to 'crop' a drawing.

This is not a technique guaranteed to redeem every unsuccessful drawing, but it can work with some drawings that have run into problems with large, uninteresting or repetitive areas. An unexciting, large drawing can sometimes make two exciting small ones!

> **Insight**
> Before you decide to crop a drawing, are you sure you cannot improve it in some way by further work? Check carefully.

Perspective and proportion

As explained in Chapter 4, one way of creating the illusion of a three-dimensional object on a flat sheet of paper is to work with tonal values. However, as well as drawing convincing, solid-looking individual shapes, artists also have to deal with the challenge of suggesting space, depth and distance in their pictures and assessing the relative proportions of one thing to another.

So, to make truly realistic drawings you will need to understand perspective and must learn how to check proportions, draw foreshortened shapes and imply distance through changes of scale. Also, colour and detail can play a part in making your drawings look three-dimensional. For instance, as with tonal values, strong colours and details tend to stand out and attract attention, so they are particularly suitable for the foreground shapes in a drawing. In general, to imply distance, you should gradually weaken the colours and reduce the amount of detail as you consider the shapes further back in your drawing.

PERSPECTIVE IN THEORY

Perspective is a drawing device that helps you suggest depth and space, particularly in relation to straight lines and parallel lines that go back into the distance. However, while the theory of perspective must be thoroughly understood, most artists do not draw with lots of vanishing points and parallel lines, for this would make their drawings look rather artificial and mechanical. What they learn to do instead is to draw with a consciousness of perspective – knowing what it does and how it affects certain shapes. Guidelines can sometimes help, but they need not be drawn with laser precision once you have understood what happens in perspective.

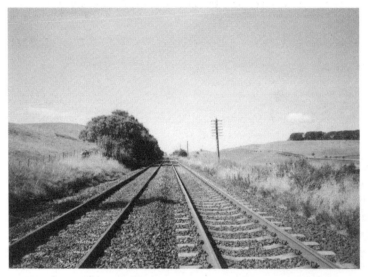

Illustration 8.10 Notice how parallel lines appear to get closer together as they go into the distance.

If you look at Illustration 8.10 you will notice that the railway lines recede into the far distance. They are parallel lines, yet they appear to converge to a distant point. This demonstrates perspective perfectly: the basic principle is that receding parallel lines appear to converge, just like the railway track. Such lines are drawn so that they taper inwards as they go back. Essentially, you are drawing exactly what you see. If you were to draw the lines as they really are, in other words keep them the same distance apart, they would look as though they were going up in the air rather than going back into the distance: vertical rather than horizontal.

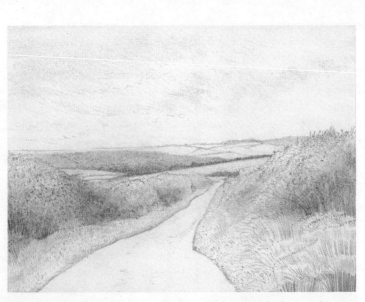

Illustration 8.11 Even when you are drawing a winding country lane you need to be aware of perspective. Notice how the edges of the lane are drawn so that they get closer together as they recede. This gives a good feeling of distance. Pencil.

The country lane drawing in Illustration 8.11 is based on the same principle. Although in reality the sides of the road are not exactly parallel, they are more or less so, and the theory of perspective applies. Consequently, the edges of the lane are drawn so that they get closer together as they recede. This gives a convincing feeling of distance.

This point is further demonstrated in Illustrations 8.12 and 8.13. In the first, the box is drawn with its sides the same width from front to back, which makes the top and bottom edges parallel. This is known as an isometric drawing – useful for designers, who need to give accurate measurements. However, in such drawings there is no sense of depth – in fact, the sides have an optical distortion that makes them look bigger at the back. In Illustration 8.13 on the other hand, the box is drawn in perspective, and in consequence the sides taper slightly as they go back. This gives a much more realistic sense of form and depth. Notice that vertical lines are unaffected by perspective.

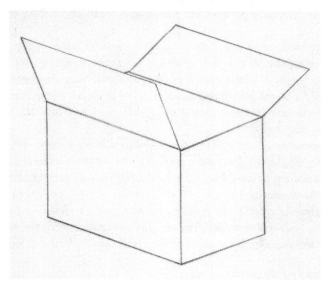

Illustration 8.12 Isometric drawing of a box.

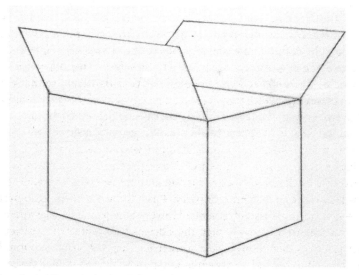

Illustration 8.13 Perspective drawing of a box.

In connection with perspective, you should get to know these terms:

▶ **Eye level** – *The actual or imagined horizontal line in a drawing that represents your line of vision in relation to the subject, i.e. the height at which your eyes observe the subject. To check this, hold a pencil horizontally about 20 cm in front of your eyes.*
▶ **Horizon** – *This is always at eye level – the line where sky meets ground.*
▶ **Converging lines** – *Parallel lines influenced by perspective; they appear to get closer together and eventually meet.*
▶ **Vanishing point** – *The point where the lines of perspective seem to meet.*
▶ **Centre of vision** – *The point on the horizon immediately in front of you as you make the drawing. This is not necessarily the middle of the drawing, because your viewpoint could be from one side.*

PERSPECTIVE IN ACTION

You can see how perspective affects the shape of things by studying Illustrations 8.14 and 8.15. In Illustration 8.14, the table is drawn in what is known as 'one-point' or 'parallel' perspective. Our viewpoint is directly on to one side and from the centre of that side. Note that lines in the drawing that are parallel to the edges of the drawing paper (that is, horizontal and vertical lines) remain parallel and unaffected by perspective, which only influences receding lines. Therefore, only the two ends of the table are affected, causing the size of the back legs and the far side to appear smaller than those parts nearer to us.

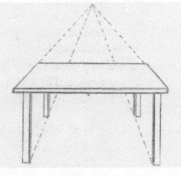

Illustration 8.14 One-point perspective drawing of a table.

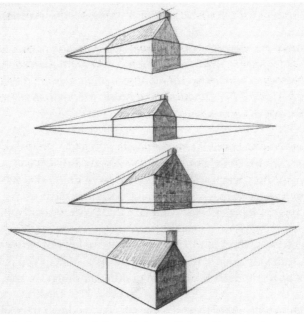

Illustration 8.15 Perspective views of a house: (a) close-up; (b) distant; (c) worm's-eye view; (d) bird's-eye view.

Now consider the alternative views of the house shown Illustration 8.15. Here we can see two sides of an object set at an angle to us. Both sides slope back from us into the distance and therefore both are influenced by perspective – in this case what is called 'angular' or 'two-point' perspective. We have two sets of converging lines, with each set meeting at a vanishing point on the horizon or eye-level line. Look at each sketch in turn:

▶ **Close-up view** *8.15(a)* – *Here the viewpoint is from normal eye level, but quite close to the building. The depth of the building is contracted or foreshortened and has to be suggested in a very limited space. The distortion of the sides is thus enhanced and the vanishing points consequently quite near the object.*

▶ **Distant view** *8.15(b)* – *The further back we stand, the less distortion there is: the sides slope back at less of an angle.*

▶ **Worm's-eye view** *8.15(c)* – *If you squat down or take a very low viewpoint, your eye level/horizon is consequently lower.*

The angle of the converging lines of perspective get steeper the further they are above the horizon.

▶ **Bird's-eye view** *8.15(d) – Similarly, if you look from a tall building or the top of a ladder, or work at an easel looking down on a still life group, your viewpoint is from above and the eye-level line is consequently high. You will, therefore, see more of the tops of objects.*

The best way to appreciate these points is to make some drawings of your own. Exercise 2 on page 138 will give you some ideas. Remember that perspective only applies to an object that has straight lines or parallel sides running back into the distance. This could be a building, a brick wall, an arch, a gate, a road, and so on.

Normally you won't need to draw the precise lines of perspective, but instead you could rely on a few guidelines to help you judge the correct angles and the relative size of different things. In fact, if you were to construct every drawing accurately, as in Illustration 8.15, then you would either have to scale the objects down tremendously in order to fit all the vanishing points on your paper, or you would have to use enormous sheets of paper! But where you have a subject which is obviously influenced by perspective, give some thought as to how lines converge and how this will help you suggest depth and relative scale. See also Illustrations 8.16 and 8.19.

Insight

Although understanding perspective is important, don't worry if you are slightly confused to begin with. The more you draw, the more you will understand when perspective is an influence.

COMPARING SHAPES AND SIZES

Imagine the edges of your sheet of drawing paper as a kind of window frame or the proscenium arch of the theatre. The viewer will look into your drawing in the same sort of way. Therefore, you have to create the illusion of space and depth. Like the set of a traditional stage play or the backdrops of a music hall, think

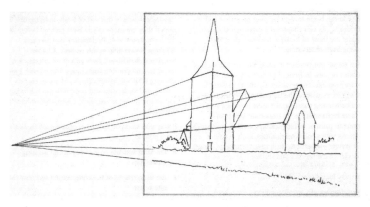

Illustration 8.16 Assessing lines of perspective is always important, but remember that the vanishing point will often be outside the picture area.

of your drawing as having a series of vertical, receding picture planes. So, as you build up the drawing, you need to be constantly aware of how the part you are working on relates to the rest of the composition. You must get each part of the drawing in the right scale and the right place. Therefore, you must make frequent cross-references.

One way of checking relative sizes and positions is to use your pencil as a measuring stick. Hold your pencil at arm's length and keep your arm straight. With one eye closed, line up the pencil with the edge, distance or angle you wish to check. Align your pencil so that its end corresponds to one end of the distance to be measured, using your thumb to mark the other end. Keeping your arm straight, you can now compare this measurement or angle with one somewhere else in the composition. In this way you can make a series of comparative checks and measurements to help you draw things in the correct relative scale.

An alternative is to use a viewfinder that incorporates a grid, see page 123 and Illustration 8.8. Hold the viewfinder at arm's length in one hand while you map in the essential lines of your drawing using the other hand. You may need to have smaller or larger viewfinders depending on the subject matter and the scale of working.

CHECKING PROPORTIONS

With many subjects, such as the human figure, it is essential to
estimate the scale of one part correctly in relation to the rest – in
other words, to check that it is in the right proportions. So try to
get into the habit of looking at things in this way and noticing
whether one part is bigger or smaller than another, and if so by
how much. If you wish, use the pencil measuring technique to
compare different sizes (see page 133).

As you gain experience you will begin to assess proportions
automatically in the way that you look and analyze. The more
you practise drawing something, the more you will appreciate the
proportions involved. This especially applies to the human form.
And although, of course, you cannot assume that every human
being fits a certain formula regarding scale and proportion, you can
use truths about average people as a guide.

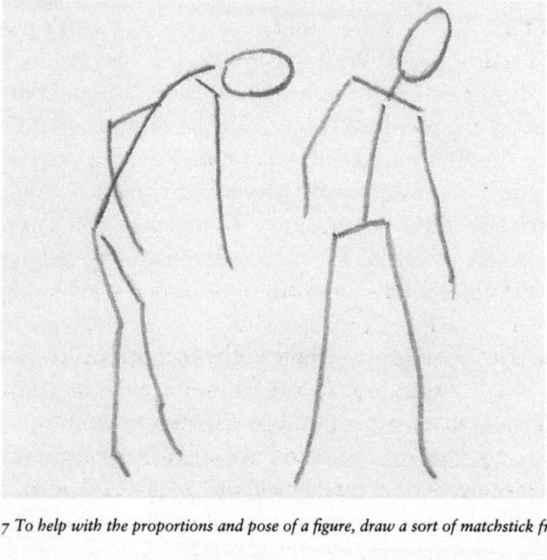

Illustration 8.17 To help with the proportions and pose of a figure, draw a sort of matchstick framework first.

For example, you may know that the height of the average person is equivalent to 7.5 heads, and that dividing the height into 'heads' helps you fix other positions and proportions. With moving figures, you might evolve the final drawing from quick matchstick or skeleton sketches, like those shown in Illustration 8.17. These can only be drawn quickly and convincingly if you have a knowledge and understanding of basic proportions. Similar points apply to drawing the head. From a profile view you will discover that the head is quite square in overall dimensions, while from a frontal view it is more rectangular. You will notice too how all the features fit into the lower half of the head. See Illustration 8.18.

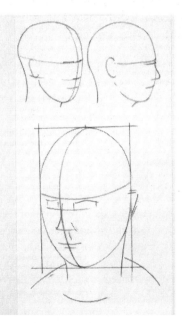

Illustration 8.18 When drawing faces and heads, check the basic proportions in this way.

Often, the overall sense of distance relies on perspective combined with the use of changing scale and proportions. And the feeling of depth can be further enhanced by the way we use tone and colour. Usually, weaker tones and colours are used in the distance and stronger ones with bolder lines for foreground detail and emphasis. Illustration 8.19 combines all of these methods and you will see that, as well as creating a good sense of depth, the various contrasts of scale and tone add interest and variety to the drawing.

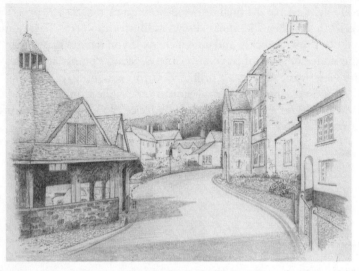

Illustration 8.19 A view of a street could involve all kinds of angles. Fix one or two 'key' shapes and then relate the others to them. Pencil.

FORESHORTENING

The position and scale of things is very important when you have to deal with an unusual or exaggerated viewpoint, such as something that juts straight out at you. In this case, because of its relative position to you, the size and shape of something may be greatly distorted or condensed, an aspect of drawing known as 'foreshortening'. So, if you want to convey a lot of distance in a very confined space, you need to use an emphasized perspective.

Look at Illustration 8.20 to see how these points apply. In the drawing on the left, the lamp is pointing away from us and consequently the lampshade is relatively small in relation to the rest because it is the furthest part from us. Contrastingly, in the right-hand drawing, the lampshade is closest to us and appears much larger.

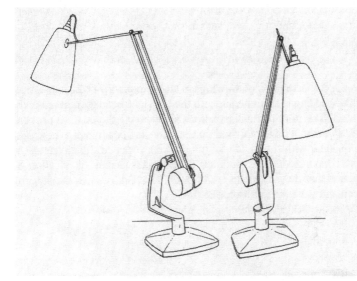

Illustration 8.20 Occasionally, you will have to deal with an exaggerated or unusual viewpoint, for example when part of an object juts straight out towards you. Notice that the lampshade on the right, which is pointing towards us, appears much larger than the one of the left, which is pointing away from us. Technical pen.

Making your drawings fit the paper

Proportions and scale also apply in a general way, of course, to the idea or composition and thus the format and size of your sheet of drawing paper. Here, some initial planning and consideration are important, otherwise you may find to your disappointment that you are well advanced with a drawing that is not going to fit your sheet of paper. In fact, in most cases you will be scaling down the subject matter to fit your drawing. This will involve keeping everything to relative proportions, while reducing the overall idea to an acceptable size.

A reliable way to work is to start from the centre of your subject matter, matching this to the centre of your drawing paper. Take one or two general measurements using the pencil or viewfinder technique described earlier in this chapter. A couple of freehand diagonal lines will give you the middle of your sheet of paper and you can gradually plan out the main shapes from there. Within your chosen subject matter, start with the object nearest the centre. Once you have estimated the proportions of this in relation to the dimensions of the complete idea, you can sketch it in based on similar proportions in relation to the size of your paper.

Insight

Sketch in the main shapes lightly and roughly at first. If everything seems to fit, go back and check proportions and shapes more carefully. If the size of your preliminary shapes were too big or too small, then obviously you can adjust them accordingly.

Exercises

1 *Using a cardboard viewfinder, go round the house and look for interesting corners and subjects to draw. Experiment with different viewpoints and with both 'portrait' and 'landscape' formats. Make composition roughs of six different ideas. Evaluate the ideas and decide which composition works best. Enlarge it into a fully worked drawing.*

2 *Take an ordinary cardboard box, such as a breakfast cereal box. Place it on a table, on its side or upright but at an angle and about 1 metre away from you. Make three outline drawings from different viewpoints. Next, place the box on the ground and try a bird's-eye view perspective drawing. Refer to Illustrations 8.13–8.15.*

3 *Ask someone to stand in an open doorway so that you can also see into the room beyond. Taking the doorframe as the boundaries for your drawing, make a drawing of the figure and anything seen in the background. Aim for a drawing that gives a good sense*

of space and depth. Use the doorframe to help you check the size and proportions of the figure and also relate its scale to the objects beyond.

4 *In your sketchbook, and working on location from an actual example, make a drawing of part or the whole of a stone or brickwork bridge. Choose a viewpoint that shows some of the underneath of the arches. Try a colour drawing technique such as pencil and wash for this project.*

10 THINGS TO REMEMBER

1 *Design, or composition, refers to the way that you arrange the different elements that you want to include in your drawing.*

2 *Start with some small, quick sketches to help you plan the design.*

3 *Think about the contrast between sizes, shapes and spaces, as well as movement and direction in the design, and try to avoid basic divisions which will make it too balanced or symmetrical.*

4 *Use lines and shapes that lead to a main focal point or centre of interest in your drawing.*

5 *In a good design, there will be no lines and shapes that lead the eye out of the picture area.*

6 *With certain shapes and types of subject matter, you may need to consider perspective in order to suggest a convincing sense of form and depth.*

7 *Assessing lines of perspective is always important, but remember that the vanishing point will often be outside the picture area.*

8 *As you make your drawing, remember to check the size and position of each shape in relation to the rest.*

9 *To ensure that your drawing will fit the paper, start by roughly plotting where the main shapes will come. This will give a good structure to work from.*

10 *To help focus your attention on a specific area of a complex subject, try using a simple cardboard viewfinder.*

9

....

Planning your drawing

In this chapter you will learn:
- *how to meet the aims of your drawing by adopting a planned approach*
- *how to develop a drawing through key stages.*

A balanced approach

In comparison to your sketchbook drawings, which might be made very quickly, perhaps in a matter of a few minutes, there will be other occasions when you will want to tackle larger, more ambitious projects. A complex drawing could take many hours to complete and, to ensure its success, it will obviously require some careful planning and preparation. From your initial thoughts and reference sketches you may need to work through quite a few stages to reach a successful result.

This section explains the process you will need to consider whenever you decide to make a resolved drawing of this type. However, before discussing the sort of stages that could be involved, I would like to add a word of caution. Do remember that in planning a drawing you must always strike a balance between the degree of preparation that you believe is necessary and, in contrast, the ability to work with complete spontaneity.

You won't want to proceed with an ill thought out idea that leads to frustration and disappointment. But at the same time, try to ensure that the planning doesn't stifle the vigour of the drawing. Aim for clear objectives and intentions, and make careful decisions about scale, composition, techniques and so on, but always leave something to discover and develop as the drawing progresses.

> ### Insight
> The amount of planning will vary from drawing to drawing; some drawings will need very little. Just do sufficient planning to give yourself the necessary confidence and sense of direction to make a start.

HELPFUL STAGES

Look upon planning as a means of enquiry and decision making which, in turn, will help you find the best approach to pursue in your main drawing. Familiarize yourself with all the points listed below and get used to doing a quick mental check of these prior to each drawing. Not every drawing will need to evolve through all of these stages, of course. But you should be aware of the sort of factors to consider, because these can greatly influence the way that the work develops. Eventually, you will start to follow this process of decision making automatically and more intuitively.

For large-scale projects and complex drawings, you may need to consider the following stages of working:

- ▶ **Aims** – *Your drawing is a visual statement, so what do you want to say? Think carefully about the subject matter and the sort of emphasis and impact you want to achieve. Make some rough plans and ideas.*
- ▶ **Research** – *Collect what information you need in the way of sketches and studies. Decide which media and techniques will work best for the effects you want.*
- ▶ **Composition** – *Make some composition roughs to try out alternative ideas before finalizing the design.*

▶ **Preparation** – *The paper may need stretching or preparing in some other way. Check that you have all the equipment and materials you will need to complete the drawing.*

CLEAR OBJECTIVES

Whatever the subject matter, you will find that you work more positively and successfully if you are trying to create something specific and have well-defined aims. If you know what you are trying to achieve in the drawing, you are more likely to achieve it! Your aim could be to make a carefully observed and detailed study of something, or you could choose a more emotional approach, such as expressing your response to a stormy seascape. Equally, the focus could be on examining the relationship of shapes and tones in a particular subject, for example, or perhaps concerned instead with a special technique or medium. It will set you a problem and channel your attention in a certain direction.

To help you decide on the best strategy for a drawing, it is a good idea to begin with some simple sketches or 'roughs'. These need only involve a few succinct lines. You can make them in your sketchbook or, if you prefer, complete the entire sequence on a large sheet of paper so that you can easily compare one to another. Use any quick sketching media, such as pencils, pastels, charcoal or felt-pens.

You can use roughs to:

▶ **get you started** – *Roughs can be used as a means of thinking on paper, brainstorming and experimenting with basic ideas.*
▶ **help you understand** – *Preliminary sketches will help you to familiarize yourself with the subject matter before tackling it in detail.*
▶ **select and compose** – *A series of quick sketches will enable you to identify the most interesting part of a complex subject, which in consequence will be the area to focus on in the main drawing. Alternatively, try a sequence of small sketches to explore different design and composition alternatives.*

▶ **experiment** – *Use simple sketches to test out the suitability of a medium for a particular idea or effect, or to check the compatibility of medium and paper or of different combinations of media.*

Insight

Having set yourself a clear objective for the drawing, try to keep to it. While you are drawing you might think of different ways, better ways of interpreting the subject, but save these for other drawings.

REFERENCE INFORMATION

Your sketchbook will be useful for more specific studies and research, especially when time and practical considerations prevent the main drawing being made on the spot. For example, this might apply with complex scenes, when travelling or on holiday somewhere, with subjects that are moving or changing in some way, and for composite ideas – when adopting a more imaginative approach incorporating ideas from a number of different sources.

If you wanted to make a convincing drawing of a bustling crowd at the races, for example, the best approach would be to start with sketches and photographs. Then, at a later date at home, with reference to the sketches and photographs, you could work on the main drawing, devoting to it whatever amount of time and thought is necessary.

For further advice and information on location sketching, see pages 108–110. Your research could be in the form of:

▶ **location drawings** – *Use your sketchbook and make some drawings on the spot to give you a general idea as well as specific information about details, textures and features.*

- ▶ **preliminary studies** – *Investigate different viewpoints, the sort of design and composition you want, and any 'awkward' parts of the subject before you begin the main drawing.*
- ▶ **using photographs and books** – *This might be essential for imaginative ideas where first-hand reference is not possible. Remember that this sort of material is for reference rather than copying.*
- ▶ **inspiration from other artists** – *Visit galleries and exhibitions to view drawings by well-known artists. Books and videos will also provide information. Studying the work of other artists is another way of increasing your knowledge and understanding of drawing and helping with your own ideas and technical problems.*

Look at Illustrations 9.1–9.3. Together these provide sufficient information from which to make a final, detailed study. The location drawings give two alternative compositions as well as some tonal reference, while the photograph is a useful reminder about other details.

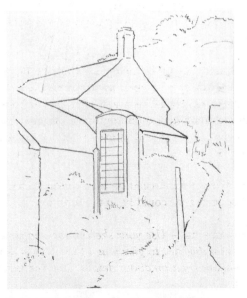

Illustration 9.1 Location sketch defining the general composition. Pen and ink.

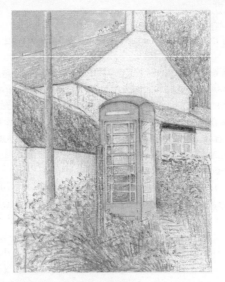

Illustration 9.2 Location sketch for tonal reference. Pencil.

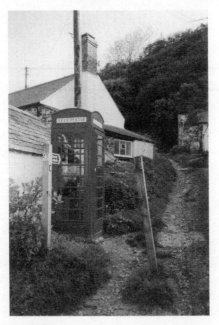

Illustration 9.3 Location photograph.

Enlarging and reducing ideas

Quite often, the main drawing is worked up from a much smaller composition sketch and therefore it is important to ensure that the larger sheet of paper is in proportion to the smaller. The quickest way of doing this is to position the sketch on the larger sheet of paper so that the bottom edge of the sketch and its left-hand side are aligned exactly with those of the big sheet. If you now place a long straight-edge diagonally across the sketch from bottom left to top right you can extend this diagonal across the larger sheet of paper. Any rectangle constructed with its top right-hand corner on this diagonal will be in proportion to the original sketch. See Illustration 9.4. You can, of course, scale down ideas by simply reversing the process.

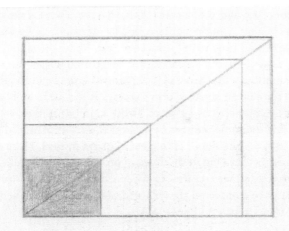

Illustration 9.4 Enlarging in proportion. Any rectangle constructed on the extended diagonal will be in proportion to the original shape (the shaded area).

It is not always necessary to enlarge the rough idea very accurately, although naturally you will want to get the general shapes and proportions approximately correct in the larger drawing. A reliable method is to start with some guidelines drawn diagonally across the sheet of paper, combining these lines with others made by dividing the paper in half in each direction. Do this with faint lines on both the sketch and the large sheet of drawing paper. Now, looking at the sketch, you can see where the main lines and shapes of the drawing come in relation to these guidelines, and so you should be able to match them to the corresponding positions on the larger sheet.

Insight

If you do not want to damage your sketch by adding guidelines or a grid across it, cover it with tracing paper and mark this instead.

SQUARING-UP

For greater accuracy, use the squaring-up method shown in Illustrations 9.5 and 9.6. Draw a grid of squares across the original drawing (or on tracing paper covering it). Measure along each side to work out how many squares to use. Make the squares a reasonable size – avoid an excessively large number, as this will unduly complicate the process. If the drawing does not divide into an exact number of squares, don't worry, as the same will happen to the proportionally larger sheet. Draw a similar grid on the large sheet, using the same number of squares in each direction. Look at the original sketch and, taking each square in turn, redraw the part of the drawing in that square on a larger scale to fit the corresponding square on the big sheet. Carry on with this process until you have completed the enlarged outline. You can then erase the unwanted faint grid lines.

Insight

Only use the squaring-up method when it is essential to have complete accuracy in enlarging an image. Often it will not matter if the larger drawing is a little bit different to the original – in fact it can be important to make some changes.

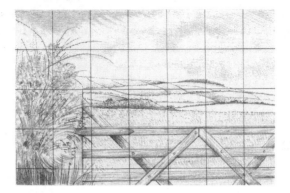

Illustration 9.5 Squaring-up a drawing.

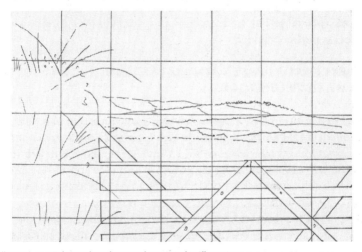

Illustration 9.6 Enlarging from the squared-up original in Illustration 9.5.

Preparing the paper

Some artists like to have the paper loose on the drawing board so that they can twist it round and get at the drawing easily from any angle. Others prefer the paper pinned to the board or held with board clips or bulldog clips. Remember to use paper that is sufficiently large so as to allow for a margin around the edge of your drawing area – this gives scope for mounting the drawing if required for framing or presentation.

Any sheet of paper that is going to be wetted in the process of completing the drawing (for example by the application of washes of tone or colour) will need stretching. This will stop the paper drying in an uneven, wrinkled state. The exception is heavy quality watercolour paper.

If all you wish to do is lightly tint the drawing here and there with a little wash, then you need only 'dry-stretch' the paper – fix the dry paper to the drawing board with a strip of gummed tape along each edge. For wetter techniques, you will need to follow the process outlined below.

PREPARING PAPER FOR BRUSH AND WASH TECHNIQUES

The paper must be of a size which will allow a margin of at least 4 cm all round on the drawing board. You will need a strip of 10 cm gummed tape for each side of the paper, cut to a length that is about 10 cm longer than the paper.

1 *Dip the paper in clean water so that both sides are wetted.*
2 *Quickly position the paper on the drawing board. Remove any surface water with a sponge, keeping the paper as flat as possible.*
3 *Again working quickly, apply the wetted gummed strips to the four edges of the paper, such that half the width of the strip adheres to the paper and half to the drawing board. If necessary, use a wet sponge to press the tape in place. However, if the paper begins to wrinkle, let the tape follow the wrinkles – don't force it flat, or it may crease.*
4 *Allow the paper to dry in a flat position at room temperature.*

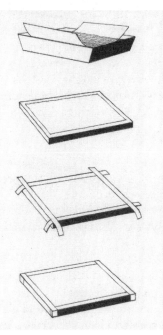

Illustration 9.7 Stages of stretching paper for use with wash and other wet techniques: (a) wetting the paper; (b) placing the wet paper flat on a drawing board; (c) using strips of brown gummed paper to tape down the edges; (d) leaving the paper to dry.

Insight

Usually, after stretching the paper, you will want to leave it to dry out completely. However, for softer, more diffused, atmospheric lines and effects, try working on the paper while it is still slightly damp.

You may want a general background tone or colour for your drawing. This can be done by dry-tinting with pastel or charcoal, working the shaded medium into the surface of the paper with a sponge. Alternatively, you can lay a wash over the whole area using diluted ink or paint applied with a very large brush or a sponge. See Illustration 9.8.

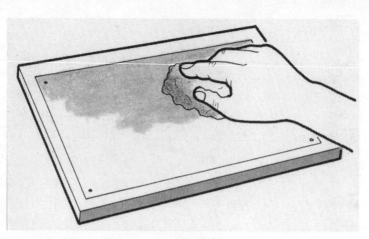

Illustration 9.8 Preparing the paper with a mid-tone by rubbing in some charcoal with a cloth.

THINKING AHEAD

At the start of each major project, you will need to make an assessment of your aims for the drawing and decide how these are going to be realized. You will also have to consider, with regard to the intended approach and outcome for the work, which techniques and media you should use, and also which paper or support to work on. Some projects will need just a few quick sketches to resolve the idea and composition, while others may require extensive research and preparation. Whatever the complexity of the proposed project, some preliminary thoughts and planning will normally prove a very worthwhile introduction to the idea, will identify any likely problems, and will establish a sense of purpose and suitable objectives to strive for.

Illustrations 9.9–9.11 show the sort of evolutionary stages that may be necessary when contemplating a resolved drawing of this type.

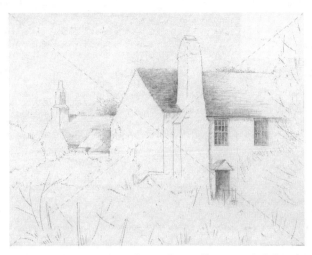

Illustration 9.9 House study. Stage 1: Plotting the main shapes and beginning to think about the strength and distribution of the different tones.

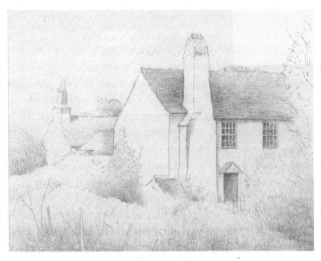

Illustration 9.10 House study. Stage 2: Establishing the tonal values.

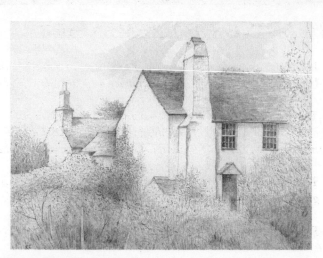

Illustration 9.11 House study. Stage 3: Developing the drawing with further tonal contrasts and details. Pencil.

Exercises

1 *Take the theme of ruins or derelict buildings. Compile some reference material in the form of location sketches, photographs and other visual reference. Work from these to produce a large, well-resolved drawing on an A2 sheet of paper which uses contrasts of tone or colour to add to the drama and impact of the idea.*

2 *Try a series of preliminary studies of a cat, dog or other pet. Work from different viewpoints, spending about ten minutes on each drawing. Get as much information as you can, including colour reference, and especially note particular features and characteristics. Use these to make one larger, well-finished study in colour.*

3 *Alternatively, work from a human model, relating the figure to the background. Follow the same procedure as in exercise 2, starting with preliminary sketches and working towards a more resolved drawing in colour.*

10 THINGS TO REMEMBER

1 For major drawing projects, some preliminary planning will help you work with greater confidence and success.

2 Think about what you hope to achieve in your drawing and also consider what you need in the form of reference information, drawing materials and so on before you can start.

3 To help you decide on the best strategy for a drawing, it is a good idea to begin with some simple sketches or 'roughs'.

4 Remember to use your sketchbook to help you plan ideas and gather the necessary reference information.

5 You can enlarge an idea from a preliminary sketch by using the squaring-up method.

6 You may need to prepare the paper in a certain way before starting your drawing, particularly if you are going to use colour wash techniques.

7 Check that you have the most appropriate type of paper for the sort of techniques and effects you want to use.

8 From your initial thoughts and reference sketches you may need to work through quite a few stages to reach a successful result.

9 Whatever degree of planning is necessary, try to ensure that it does not diminish the vigour and impact of the drawing.

10 Gradually, as you gain some experience with planning and decision making you will begin to work more automatically and intuitively.

10

Subject matter

In this chapter you will learn:
- *how to choose your subject matter*
- *key points about drawing landscape and still life subjects*
- *key points about drawing other types of subject matter.*

What to draw

Look for varied, challenging subjects: draw anything and everything! Naturally you will have your own views about suitable subject matter, but avoid the temptation to play safe all the time, so that you only concentrate on those subjects that you know you can draw well. Instead, you might be moved by the drama of a sweeping landscape or the subtleties of light and dark in a group of objects, the excitement and bustle at a busy railway station or the quiet simplicity of a corner of your garden. The scope is boundless – there are ideas everywhere.

The danger in repeating an idea is that it will lack the inspiration and challenge that you found in it initially, and therefore the result will be less successful. Once you have said all you can about a subject, why draw it again? An important factor is that the subject or theme excites and interests you. Remember too that the chosen viewpoint, medium and technique all play their part in creating a certain impact, and that the aims for the drawing will depend on those qualities within the subject matter that most impress you. However, you do not need to aim for total accuracy and realism.

Inspiration

You will find ideas and inspiration in the most unlikely places. Look at the range of ideas shown in Illustrations 10.1–10.6, for example. Possibly not all of these subjects will appeal to you, but they do indicate the variety of things that you could draw and the different methods and media that can be used. With some subjects it could be the relationship of shapes and tones that attracts you, while with others you might see the potential for using a certain medium, approach or technique. You could decide to make a detailed study of part of a very complex form, or find that simple, commonplace subjects also inspire lively drawings.

You are more likely to make a good drawing if the subject is something that you really want to draw rather than one you feel you ought to draw. Perhaps you have particular interests and hobbies that will create opportunities and ideas for drawings. In fact, a fascination with and good knowledge of your subject matter will help you draw it more convincingly. For example, if you are a keen long-distance walker or a Grand Prix enthusiast, take along your sketchbook and collect some ideas to develop.

We have seen that artists draw almost anything and that the classification of subject matter can range from detailed realism to abstract, and embrace ideas developed from fantasy and imagination through to various interpretations of natural forms, still lifes, landscapes, figures and portraits. As well as from your own thoughts, ideas and sketches, you might be inspired by the work, techniques and subject matter of other artists, or find general ideas to develop from photographs and similar visual aids. To begin with, try to gain a wealth of experience by attempting as many different types of subject matter and ideas as you can – there are all kinds of exciting things to draw.

Here are some points to bear in mind when drawing different types of subject matter.

LANDSCAPES

There are two main types of landscape subjects: the general view and the smaller, more intimate scene. Each landscape has its own special sense of place and, as well as aiming to capture this (from observation and deciding which qualities are the most important), the other key consideration is how to achieve a convincing feeling of space and depth.

Success with this aspect of landscape drawing relies mainly on understanding how the scale, tonal values, colours and degree of detail are influenced by their relative distance from you, together with the influence of light and atmosphere. Figures in different parts of the scene will suggest changes of scale, for example, while a receding fence or row of trees will have an inherent perspective, leading the eye further into the distance and so indicating the extent of the space involved.

Far off colours appear to acquire a bleached quality; they are weaker in tone and colour intensity. And as for detail, the nearest objects are naturally the ones that are seen, and therefore drawn, in the sharpest focus. Usually, the drawing in the foreground will be more considered. In the distance, shapes such as trees and field barns might be defined in part, but with other areas 'lost' against the background. See Illustrations 10.1 and 10.2, and Plates 4, 5, 10, 15 and 24.

> ### Insight
> There is nothing quite like working outside, especially on a fine, warm day, but changing light and weather can make things difficult sometimes. Be prepared to adjust your hopes and aspirations to suit the conditions. For example, sometimes it is wiser to make a sequence of quick sketches rather than try a more complex, resolved drawing.

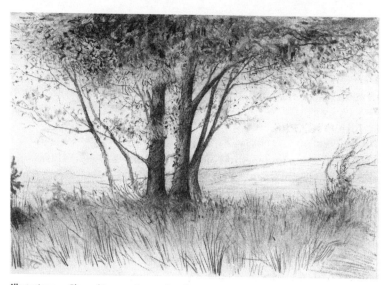

Illustration 10.1 Charcoal is an excellent medium for capturing the various qualities of a landscape subject.

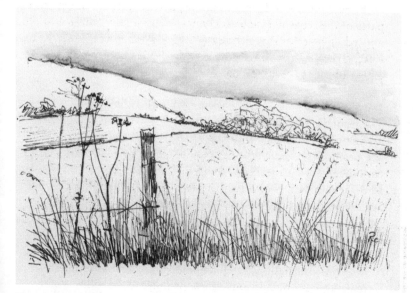

Illustration 10.2 If time is limited, concentrate on the main elements and qualities of a landscape scene. Pen and ink with ink wash.

STILL LIFE

One advantage of still life is that you have total control over the content of the drawing and can decide exactly how the various objects are arranged, lit and so on. However, there is always the risk that this type of still life will look rather contrived and make it difficult to create a drawing that has feeling and originality. Ideally, like any form of drawing, a still life must offer something individual and challenging to the viewer, and there are various ways of doing this. You can ensure that the selected objects are interesting and the composition exciting; you can involve bold colour or adopt an unusual viewpoint or form of lighting; or you can create interest through the choice of medium or technique. A good way to help decide which approach will work best is to make a sequence of small sketches that you can compare and analyze.

Especially with still life subjects, the presence of light and shade will add a further, interesting dimension, and it also helps to link the different objects together and create a feeling of space and form. Instead of focusing solely on the objects, another way to create interest is to take a much wider viewpoint and include part of the room or the window behind.

Also, you could try a 'found' still life group, which could involve objects of a much larger scale and so encourage a sense of freedom and spontaneity in the drawing. Look around your house or in the garden to see if you can find an interesting corner or group of objects to draw, as in Illustration 10.3. Objects that have been placed together quite by chance often make a much more successful and challenging arrangement to draw.

Insight
You will find lots of interesting things in your home which you can draw either as individual objects or in groups, and this is a good way to gain some confidence and skills.

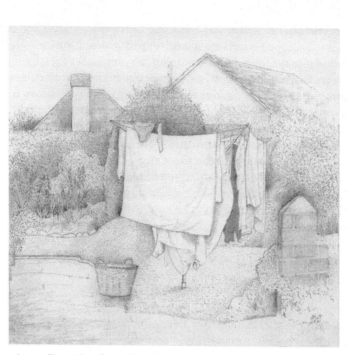

Illustration 10.3 You won't need to search very far for subjects to draw – they are all around you. Even an everyday scene such as this can make a challenging and interesting drawing. Pencil.

BUILDINGS AND INTERIORS

As well as involving a play of shapes and tones, buildings and interiors offer lots of scope for working with different textures. Again, these are subjects that can be tackled as general views or by focusing on something more specific, such as a façade, part of an interior, or even just a particularly interesting window or doorway.

There are two main points to bear in mind. The first is that many buildings and interiors are quite complex, perhaps with a tremendous amount of architectural detail. Therefore, inevitably any drawing must involve a degree of simplification. So, aim for the essential character of the subject rather than specific detail: look for features that identify the particular building and concentrate on those.

The second point is that buildings and interiors invariably include straight lines, objects placed at an angle to you and similar structural and design elements. Such lines and angles are obviously important and consequently it is often assumed that they must be drawn very accurately and with a knowledge and application of perspective. An awareness of perspective is necessary, of course, but try not to be too rigid in its application and certainly avoid the use of any form of straight edge. The drawing must look right, but at the same time it can convey a degree of expression and spontaneity. See Illustration 10.4 and Plate 20.

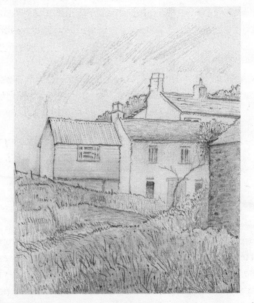

Illustration 10.4 Although buildings must look right, this need not exclude expression and spontaneity in the drawing. Pencil.

GARDENS AND FLOWERS

A garden does not have to be elaborate and full of exotic plants to be worthy of a drawing. A corner of an allotment can be just as inspiring. You could draw in your own garden or that of a friend, or visit large public gardens or country house gardens to find ideas. A garden scene could also include a part of a building, an abandoned wheelbarrow, a table and chairs, a basket or some other item that suggests a human presence and creates a focus of interest.

For individual flower studies you could try a detailed tonal drawing, as in Illustration 10.5, or place the emphasis on colour. Pastels and water-soluble coloured pencils are ideal media to use. There are various methods of approach, from making very accurate studies of flowers, perhaps in the manner of a botanical illustrator, to drawing in a more expressive way and tackling flowers in a general or 'found' context, such as in pots and hanging baskets, as well as set arrangements. Careful observation is the key to success with leaf and petal shapes, proportions and other characteristics.

Insight

Gardens can be very difficult, complex subjects, but as with other subjects, think initially in terms of the main shapes and masses. And only add detail where it is vital to the sense and impact of the drawing.

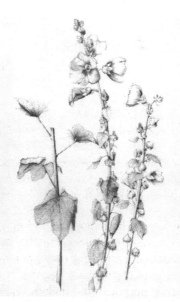

Illustration 10.5 Flowers make wonderful subjects for a highly resolved drawing such as this. Pencil.

SKIES AND WATER

Skies can be very dramatic and make interesting studies in their own right, while in a landscape subject it is usually the sky that is the most influential area in terms of light, and thus in determining a certain mood for the drawing. When drawing landscapes, it is a good idea to start with the sky and establish the principal tonal qualities and characteristics here, and then build up the rest of the drawing in relation to this area. Recommended media include charcoal, which will give many variations of tone and can be lifted-out and modified with a putty eraser, and for colour studies, pastel, which has similar properties.

Like skies, water is something in which the influence of light is very obvious. This being so, water can vary considerably in its character and appearance. Although it often looks transparent, there are usually the added problems of reflections and the fact that it is moving – both of which are difficult qualities to express in a drawing. Before attempting your drawing, spend a few minutes studying the water and noting its particular characteristics – whether it is smooth, rippled, rough, dark, light or so on. From this analysis you will be able to decide which tones/colours and types of marks will be the most suitable to help you depict the characteristics effectively.

FIGURES

Pose, proportion and character are vital qualities to address when making a carefully observed figure study or portrait. However, in most drawings figures play a supporting rather than a principal role, and therefore, while scale and pose remain important, the emphasis will be on suggesting the stance, movement and narrative element of the figures, rather than a concern for detail. Figures will give weight to a composition and add interest and impact. They are a good device to attract the viewer's attention and direct it around the drawing.

Figures are certainly one of the most difficult subjects to sketch and paint. The main thing is to trust your eyes rather than your knowledge of figures, and to concentrate on the basic shapes, proportions and angles. Use your sketchbook to capture various poses and different types of figures – people walking, running, drinking coffee, shopping, standing in groups and so on. Try working quickly in line and tone, using a pencil or pen. When incorporating figures into a drawing, remember to check the size of each one in relation to its surroundings and, of course, in relation to figures in other parts of the drawing. See Plate 22.

Insight

Don't be afraid to draw figures just because they are difficult. Get a friend or member of your family to sit or stand in different positions for short poses for you, so that you can practise.

SHADOWS AND REFLECTIONS

As well as being significant as a means of defining form and suggesting a certain mood and quality of light, shadows can be an important compositional element. Indeed, sometimes it is the shadows themselves that have the most impact within the drawing. Foreground shadows are particularly useful in this respect. They can help define and describe areas that are lacking in specific features and, as far as the composition is concerned, they can lead the eye into the drawing, directing our attention towards the main area of interest.

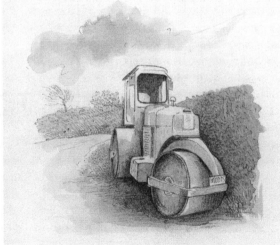

Illustration 10.6 Shadows always add to the interest of a subject. Pencil and wash.

To help yourself draw shadows convincingly, start by carefully observing the source of each one and noting its direction, strength (tone or colour) and shape. If you are drawing in colour, don't assume that shadows are simply grey or some kind of dark colour. Their colour will be influenced by the surface on which they fall and it will reflect to some extent the surrounding colours. Moreover, shadows are seldom just flat areas of colour. Look closely and you will find that they contain variations of colour and tone.

Like shadows, reflections can contribute in a very positive way to the composition, and also similarly, they must relate convincingly to the parent object. Generally, reflections should be considered as an integral part of the water surface rather than an effect that is superimposed afterwards. Reflections are, in fact, water influenced by other shapes and colours. Again, rely on your observation: you will notice, for example, that in moving water the reflections are broken in outline and somewhat distorted, whereas in calm water they can appear almost as an exact mirror-image.

Exercises

1 *Look at the drawings throughout this book and select three different themes for drawings of your own. Work in a colour medium for at least one of your drawings.*

2 *Find a subject in which shadows play a major part in creating interest and impact. Make a large, freely expressed drawing in charcoal.*

3 *Working in colour, make a careful drawing of a small group of flowers, and then a quick sketch of part of a garden.*

10 THINGS TO REMEMBER

1 *Add to your experience by trying as many different types of subject matter and ideas as you can.*

2 *With every subject, decide which are the most important qualities to focus on and aim to express those in an interesting, individual way.*

3 *Don't just draw things that are within your 'comfort zone'. Be ambitious!*

4 *You are more likely to make a successful drawing if the subject is something that inspires you to draw it, rather than something you feel you ought to draw.*

5 *Remember that the chosen viewpoint, medium and technique will all play their part in helping to achieve a certain impact in the drawing.*

6 *Getting to know the subject matter – over a period of time and by making lots of drawings – will help you understand it and, in consequence, be able to draw it more convincingly.*

7 *Subjects for drawings include landscapes, still life, buildings and interiors, skies and water, gardens and flowers, and figures.*

8 *Still life can be a good type of subject matter to begin with, because it gives you total control over the content, lighting and composition for the drawing.*

9 *Pay particular attention to the lighting, shadows and reflections in your drawings, if necessary emphasizing tonal contrasts to add impact.*

10 *Try colour as well as black and white techniques.*

11

Developing your ability

In this chapter you will learn:
- *what is meant by style*
- *how to work from memory and imagination*
- *how to make abstract drawings*
- *how to evaluate your work.*

A personal style

Drawing offers something for everyone. There is a wide choice of media, techniques and approaches and, of course, an inexhaustible supply of subject matter. Initially, it makes sense to work at gaining some experience and confidence by practising the main techniques and processes, but in time you will want to try out your own ideas and start to develop an individual way of drawing.

Reaching the point where you have a recognizable style and you are beginning to succeed in making the sort of drawings that truly reflect your ideas and feelings will take time. To draw well and to make real progress requires much perseverance and practice. Ideally you need to draw every day, even if this is only a ten-minute sketching session. Drawing is a combination of skill, perception and attitude. As well as the resolve to practise and persevere, you will also need the will to experiment and confront new ideas, and the determination to tackle problems as they occur.

Whichever direction you take or path you seek to explore, your foundation skills will give you a good starting point. In fact, for many artists these skills remain at the focus of their work and are constantly being improved. With other artists, the approach is gradually modified and developed away from formal values and the reliance on objective study and a representational outcome, although even here basic skills remain important and influential.

Style is the distinctive or characteristic way of working which identifies a particular artist. Artists like Van Gogh or Picasso, for example, have no real need to sign their work, for their signatures and personality are embodied within their drawings. Their style is immediately recognizable. In the main, artists do not set out to create a certain style – it evolves over a period of time. Your style will be the result of a combination of factors – the media and techniques you use, your subject matter, and your own personality and how you see and react to things.

Often, one of these factors dominates. An artist's drawings may be instantly recognizable because of the specific subject matter, for example, or an unusual technique. Therefore, try to be patient about style; let it grow naturally. As you pursue certain subjects, develop particular techniques, and draw with increasing freedom and confidence, so your style will gradually emerge.

Insight

The worst thing you can do is copy features from other artists' work and in this way contrive a style that you think will impress people. Be true to yourself!

VARIETY

Success in drawing relies on a breadth of experience. How else are you going to find out which subjects and techniques excite you the most? You have to test out different ideas and approaches. And inspiration isn't always a bolt from the blue! In fact, sometimes the inspiration is not the initial reaction at all, but develops during the making of the drawing as you see an unusual, clever or alternative way of progressing. Inspiration is easier for more experienced artists, because they are better able to visualize the full potential of an idea, with probably a variety of ways of drawing it. But, whatever you are drawing, try to get fully involved and excited by it. If you are excited, the drawing is likely to show it and, in return, the finished work will excite other people.

Eventually you may want to specialize and concentrate on themes and subjects that especially appeal to you, but this should grow out of a good, general understanding of drawing. You will see from this section that drawings can rely on memory and imagination as much as on observation and analysis. You may also like to try an approach that selects and organizes to create a more abstract outcome.

Drawing and discovering

Even if you have planned your work very carefully, you can never be quite sure what is going to happen once the drawing is under way. To an extent, every drawing is a journey into the unknown, a voyage of discovery, and this is exactly as it should be. What you find out during the drawing process might be something about the subject matter, about the method or medium you are using, or about yourself. And although this discovery may seem very small in itself, it will inevitably add to your wider knowledge and skills.

It follows that the more you draw, the more you will discover. And the greater the scope of your subject matter and techniques, the greater your drawing experience. So don't be afraid to attempt difficult subjects. Rather, see what you can find out by drawing them. Sometimes it is a good idea to do this by picking a subject at random. In addition, see what you can discover about different effects and techniques by trying out a new medium.

Illustrations 11.1–11.3 demonstrate the importance of the medium and technique in helping to convey particular intentions and qualities in a drawing. In these three examples you will see that, as appropriate to the subject matter, each drawing has been made with a different medium, thus enabling certain qualities and effects to be emphasized: expression and mood in Illustration 11.1; tonal variations in Illustration 11.2; and different surface qualities and textures in Illustration 11.3.

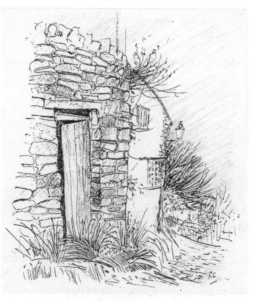

Illustration 11.1 The mood of this drawing is largely determined by the particular choice of medium and technique. Pen and ink with pencil.

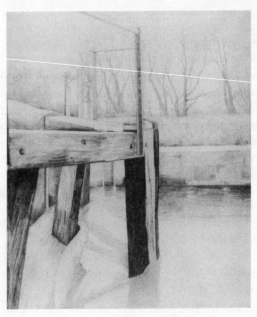

Illustration 11.2 To create the necessary tonal contrasts, pencil and charcoal were used for this drawing.

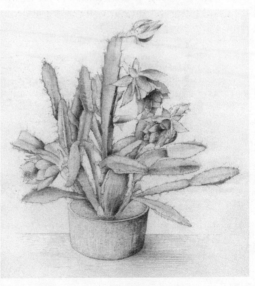

Illustration 11.3 Accuracy, detail and surface textures were important qualities to address in this drawing. Pencil.

Using your memory

Imaginative and fantasy ideas rely to some extent on working from memory and it is possible, of course, to make a drawing entirely from memory. Additionally, preliminary sketches and research drawings won't be able to contain every detail of the information you want and therefore you may have to use a certain amount of invention, experience and memorized information to complete the work.

Also, sometimes you will find that time is against you when you are out and about sketching, preventing you from completing the reference drawing, especially if it is something quite detailed, as in Illustration 11.4. Consequently, the subsequent studio drawing might need to be developed from a mixture of observed fact, areas developed from notes and other reference material, and what you can remember. See also Plate 2.

Insight

Whatever you are drawing, a little imagination or invention is usually a good thing, because it will make the drawing more personal and expressive.

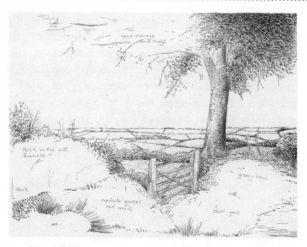

Illustration 11.4 With a detailed study there may not be enough time to finish everything on the spot and so you will also need to rely on your memory. Pen and ink.

So, as an artist, you need to train your memory; you need to have a good visual vocabulary, as it were, which you can refer to when needed. The way to improve your memory is to do plenty of observation drawings of a wide variety of subjects. Fill your sketchbooks with them. This will not only get you into the habit of drawing in such a way that you are looking, examining and understanding, but it will also mean that you are more likely to be able to recall those shapes and draw them from memory if need be.

Working from visual material

You can find images in photographs, magazines and books as the inspiration for your drawings, but you do need to be careful how you use such material. There are many artists who totally reject the idea of using second-hand imagery as source material. On the other hand, there are those who feel quite justified in relying on an enlarger or projector to project an image onto a sheet of paper so that they can draw round the outlines. There is probably a happy compromise.

Certainly, photographs can be useful from time to time. We have already seen that they can provide good back-up information in conjunction with sketches and other research drawings, especially if you want to explore different viewpoints and composition ideas or you need specific detail or colour reference. There are even occasions when the photograph could be copied – as part of a drawing where you require the exact detail, for example. But, on the whole, photographs are aids, starting points and supplementary reference: they are not for copying.

There are two main reasons why you should not directly copy a photograph. The first is that your drawing needs to be your idea and as lively and spontaneous as possible. This is difficult if you are simply reworking a photograph. Secondly, photographs often distort distance and perspective and it becomes difficult to translate something like a view down a street, for example, into a convincing drawing. Obviously this may depend on the quality of your camera and your own photography skills, but you will notice in many photographs that vertical lines frequently tilt inwards and that the perspective of buildings and similar objects is exaggerated. Equally, depending on the camera and the processing, colours can be approximate to say the least.

Your own photographs are always the best ones to use. This is because if you took the photographs, you obviously spent some time looking at the actual subject matter, and consequently any thoughts and opinions you have about it will further inform the drawing. Also, with your own photographs there are no copyright problems; if you copy someone else's photographs without their permission, and particularly if you subsequently offer the work for sale, you may be infringing their copyright.

If you make a drawing from one of your photographs, try altering the composition somewhat; use the photograph only as a reminder and a starting point. The most important thing to remember when working in this way is that you are creating a drawing – not reproducing a photograph. So you need to be sensitive to the drawing process involved. There are many other ways that photographs can be useful, such as starting points for studying tone and shape or developing a selective or abstract result, as shown in Illustration 11.5.

Insight

If you are using photographs as reference material, pin them up somewhere slightly away from where you are working – so that you can refer to them, but are not tempted to copy everything.

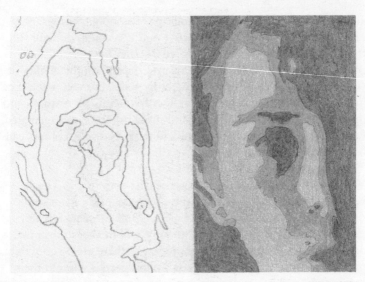

Illustration 11.5 Black and white photographs are very useful for showing general areas of tone, which can then be simplified and interpreted in an abstract way. Pencil.

Fantasy and imagination

Many artists work from imagination rather than observation: they draw from ideas in their head rather than by sitting in front of objects or a scene. Whatever our approach or style, or our philosophy towards drawing, we all need to use imagination in our work to some extent. Now and again it is good for us, and our work in general, if we can freely express ourselves in this way.

Inspiration for this sort of work might come from a number of sources: through particular interests, for example science fiction or mythology; from books, poems and films; from travel; by interpreting observed subjects in a much more personal way; from the work of other artists; or by setting yourself a theme to research and develop in an imaginative way. Think best how to use techniques and media to add to the individuality of the work and remember that you may need to exaggerate, distort or use an unusual viewpoint or context in order to create the right feeling and impact in your drawing.

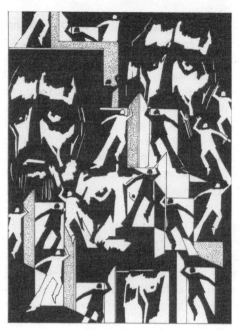

Illustration 11.6 Try some drawings that are pure fantasy and imagination. The repeated shapes in this design were made by using templates and tracings. Fibre-pen.

Abstract drawings

It is perhaps easier to see the validity and merit of creating a faithful likeness in a portrait drawing or capturing the atmosphere and feeling of a landscape view, than it is to appreciate an abstract result. But not all abstract drawings are just a collection of careless lines and random marks! In fact, many of them result from applying a particular theory, restriction or emphasis to the drawing process. You might, for example, be interested in investigating the decorative quality of an idea by reducing it to a series of outlines that are all drawn with equal emphasis. Alternatively, you could view the subject purely in terms of three tones or colours, and so on. These processes not only produce some exciting results, but are very useful drawing exercises as well.

There are three main approaches to abstract work that you may like to try: draw from observation but simplify, distort or select from what you see; use lines and geometrical shapes arranged in a deliberate composition and perhaps enhanced with tone or colour; or make random and uninhibited marks to create a free and expressive drawing. Do consider some of these approaches, because it does help your overall progress if your experience of drawing is wide ranging. Of course, in time, you will probably want to reject some techniques, styles and philosophies, but try to ensure that you do this from an informed standpoint, from a knowledge and experience of the things you are rejecting.

My drawing in Illustration 11.7 was worked from an actual subject studied objectively. But, because I have concentrated on a limited range of flat tones related to equally assessed foreground and background shapes, the result is semi-abstract. Contrastingly, I have used a collage technique in Illustration 11.8. The original drawing was cut into strips then arranged and glued to a backing sheet. Your abstracts can use an intellectual, ingenious or imaginative approach, can be fun, and at the same time can help you discover much about materials and methods. See also Plate 2.

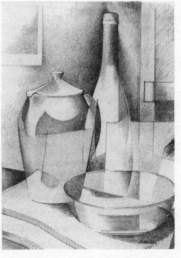

Illustration 11.7 Working with simplified shapes and flat areas of tone will give a bold, semi-abstract result, as here. Pencil.

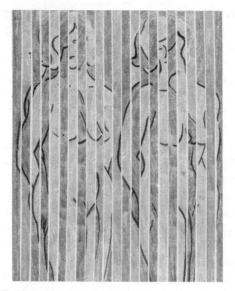

Illustration 11.8 Collage design. The original drawing was cut into strips, rearranged, and glued to a backing sheet of card. Pencil.

Evaluation

The drawing process is one in which you are constantly making judgements. You are, in effect, being self-critical all the time. For example, you will need to question whether you have made a line too long, whether something is too big, whether a shadow should be a little darker, and so on. At the end of each drawing, try to spend a few minutes looking at it and assessing its success. Does it fulfil its aims? If it is a preliminary sketch, does it provide enough information to work from? If it is the main drawing, has it got the sort of feeling, effects and impact that you were aiming for?

In addition, it is important to keep a check on your general progress and development. A periodic evaluation could take the form of a display of all your recent work. By looking at 10–20 drawings, you can make a better judgement about weaknesses in technique and the sort of things you ought to be practising more, as well as the strengths and interests you should be building on. This kind of assessment helps in making decisions about the future direction of your work and the particular aspects you should be concentrating on.

> **Insight**
>
> Keep all of your drawings for evaluation – the good and the bad. You will often learn more from the mistakes than the successes.

Constructive self-criticism isn't easy. There is a happy balance between being blasé and expecting everything to right itself, and being zealously critical to the point of abject depression! Try to justify criticisms and decide on remedies. It could simply be a matter of more practice or revision, or of seeking additional help from books, DVDs or tuition.

It can also help to get other people's opinion of your work. If you know other people who draw and sketch, get together for a shared evaluation session. Alternatively, join an art society or club, or enrol on a life class or other drawing course. This will give you the opportunity to meet other artists, both amateur and professional, and to exchange views and ideas.

Exercises

1   *Develop two drawings, on A2 sheets of paper or larger, on the theme of 'light and dark'. In the first drawing, work as much as possible from imagination and aim to express the theme in a very individual and personal way. For the second drawing, work from a still life group, making tone (and/or colour) the prime interest in your drawing. For both drawings, consider the best media to use and whether your idea would be more effective in colour or on coloured paper.*
2   *Make an evaluation of your last ten drawings. In your notebook or sketchbook, note down any obvious weaknesses and suggested remedies.*

10 THINGS TO REMEMBER

1 *A good visual memory is an asset for all artists. Help train your memory by doing as much sketching and observation drawing as you can.*

2 *You will work in a more original, individual way if you do not rely too much on photographs as reference material.*

3 *Be willing to experiment with your subject matter and perhaps try a more imaginative or abstract type of drawing now and again.*

4 *Rather than deliberately trying to create a certain style, allow your personal style to develop gradually.*

5 *Whatever you are drawing, try to get fully involved and excited by it. If you are excited, the drawing is likely to show it and, in return, the finished work will excite other people.*

6 *One of the joys of drawing is that you can never be quite sure what will happen, however well you have planned things. Often, in the process of drawing, you will discover something about the subject matter, the method or medium you are using, or perhaps about yourself!*

7 *At the end of each drawing, spend a few minutes looking at it and assessing its success. Does it fulfil its aims?*

8 *Periodically assess your general progress and take steps to improve any aspects that you think are weak.*

9 *Joining an art society, life class or other drawing course will give you the opportunity to meet other artists and exchange views and ideas.*

10 *Success in drawing depends on a combination of skill, perception and attitude.*

12

Framing and presentation

In this chapter you will learn:
- *how to prepare your drawings for framing*
- *how to choose mounts and frames*
- *how best to display your drawings.*

Selecting and preparing

Drawings are seldom made with the specific intention that the finished work will be framed and displayed. In fact, generally the reason for drawing is the sheer enjoyment of expressing an idea that interests you, or perhaps to make reference studies or development sketches, rather than exhibition pieces. However, as your work develops and you create some drawings that are particularly successful, you will naturally want to mount and frame one or two. You could display these in your home, or even exhibit them.

Choose drawings that you are really pleased with, those that show your skills to advantage – both your technical ability and powers of expression. Ideally, a drawing that is selected for framing should be one that will continue to give pleasure and interest whenever you look at it. Having selected a drawing to frame, check it over to see if there are any final details or alterations you would like to make. Clean off unwanted marks and if necessary spray the drawing with fixative. This is particularly recommended for drawings that have been made with soft, smudgy media, such as charcoal and pastel, to prevent them offsetting and spoiling.

Fixative is a type of thin varnish. It is available in aerosol containers or it can be bought in liquid form and applied with a metal spray diffuser. Spray the drawing in a well-ventilated room, from a distance of about 30 cm. Start at the top and work across and downwards. Spray lightly and allow the work to dry. Test a corner to see if the drawing will still smudge and, if so, apply a further coating of fixative. Next, trim the drawing to a size that leaves at least a 2.5 cm margin as overlap for the mount.

BACKING DRAWINGS

The way that a drawing is attached to the mount is a matter of personal preference: some artists like the drawing to hang freely within the mount and are not bothered by any slight surface undulation, while others prefer it to be absolutely flat. Large drawings, or drawings on thin paper, may need backing before fixing them to a mount. This is done by gluing the drawing to a sheet of thicker paper or card. Choose a card with a low pH value, preferably acid-neutral. Suitable types of card are available at art materials shops and framers. Use a wheat starch powder or water-soluble PVA adhesive, both of which have a neutral pH value.

For drawings that need a backing support, follow this procedure:

▶ *Choose a sheet of thin, acid-neutral card slightly larger than the frame and mount you intend using for the drawing.*
▶ *Place the drawing (which will include a slight margin around the edges as an overlap for the mount) as near as you can*

judge in the centre of the sheet of card – such that there is an equal margin top and bottom, and at both sides.

▶ *Mark the position of the drawing paper on the card with some pencil lines.*

▶ *Quickly apply a thin, even coating of adhesive to the area within your pencil lines.*

▶ *Lower the drawing in place and, again working quickly, use some off-cuts of clean paper to press down on the drawing and smooth out any wrinkles that appear. Work from the centre to the edges and press firmly.*

▶ *Place the drawing under a drawing board or similar heavy board and put a few heavy books on top for extra weight. Allow the backed drawing to dry under pressure for 24 hours.*

▶ *Take the mount you have selected and place this over the drawing. Use some double-sided tape or one or two dabs of PVA adhesive to hold the mount in place.*

▶ *Trim off any surplus backing card that shows around the edges of the mount.*

Insight

It is very important that you work quickly and that the drawing is absolutely flat on the backing support, with no wrinkles. Practise on one of your less successful drawings first.

Choosing mounts

Mounts and frames serve both a practical and an aesthetic function. Drawings need the protection of glass and, in addition, the overall style of presentation should help focus attention on the work and enhance its impact. Therefore, in your decisions about framing you need to consider the complete combination of drawing, mount and frame. You may want to mount and frame your drawings yourself, or instead you may prefer to have this work done professionally.

Whatever you decide, if possible it is a good idea to cut some strips from various types and colours of mounting card, or to make some right-angle 'L'-shape pieces (like those suggested for cropping a drawing on page 125), which you can use to try out different combinations and effects. Place them against your drawing to check which colour and type of mounting card will look best. Also, if you can beg or buy a few short lengths of different framing mouldings from your local picture framer, you can use these in conjunction with the sample mounts to get a fairly accurate impression of the combined effect of mount and frame. In your deliberations, you will need to consider whether you need to use a single, double or oval mount, as well as which colour and texture will be the most suitable.

CUTTING MOUNTS

The mount is usually cut so that it has a slightly wider margin at the bottom than at the sides or top. The width of these margins will depend on the content and impact of the drawing. As an example, an A3 drawing will need margins of about 6.5 cm, with 7.5 cm at the bottom.

You can cut a simple window mount with a sharp craft knife used against a metal straight edge. First, cut the card to fit the dimensions of the frame. Then mark off the margins of the mount on the back of the card and cut out the centre piece, or if you prefer, work from the front. As you handle and measure the card, be careful not to mark or damage it in any way. And similarly, try to ensure that all the cuts are clean and straight, with precise right angles at the corners.

Cutting from the front of the mount will usually give a neater finish. Begin by marking off the width of the side margins with faint pencil lines along the top and bottom edges, then place a Perspex rule across the card and, with a pin prick, mark the actual corners of the part to be cut out. Finally, cut out the centre shape using a very sharp knife against a metal rule, working on a cutting mat. Avoid over-cutting at the corners, which will spoil the look of the mount.

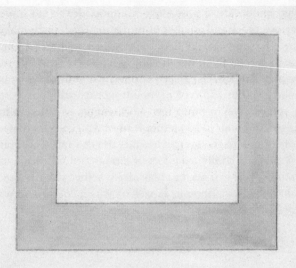

Illustration 12.1 Cut the mount so that it has a slightly wider margin at the bottom than at the sides and top.

Ideally, if you decide to make all your own mounts you will need to invest in a good quality mount cutter. This will enable you to produce professional-looking results. Mount cutters are available from artists' materials shops: ask for a demonstration. Practise on some card off-cuts first.

> **Insight**
>
> Also, many art shops stock ready-cut mounts in different colours and sizes, which you can buy and keep in stock for possible future use.

Work can also be flat-mounted, that is trimmed to the exact dimensions of the drawing and glued to a backing sheet of white or coloured card cut to a size that will give a border around the drawing, or you can use a double mount. Fix the drawing to the mount with double-sided framer's tape.

There is a huge variety of mounting cards and boards to choose from. Avoid any that are not acid-free, as these may cause some discolouration to the edges of the mounted work over a period of time. There are also problems with the lightfast quality of some cards. Ideally you should use a good quality neutral pH board, such as Daler Studland Board. Similarly, where work is taped to the back of a mount, an acid-free framing tape should be used.

If you lack the time, confidence or equipment to have a go yourself, then discuss any ideas for mounting and framing your drawings with a professional framer.

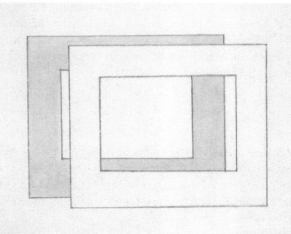

Illustration 12.2 Some drawings will benefit from the use of a double mount. This usually has a narrow inner strip (perhaps measuring 5–10 mm) of a slightly contrasting colour to the main outer border. Similarly, a stepped effect, using the same coloured mount board for both inner and outer mounts, can look interesting. Double mounts often give a more pleasing, professional look and another advantage is that the narrow inner mount will form a useful defining and unifying edge to the drawing. Use double-sided framer's tape to fix the two mounts together.

Choosing frames

Like mounts, frames need to be of a high quality if they are to complement the drawing to the best effect. You may be interested in buying all the necessary equipment and making your own frames. Alternatively, you can have frames made to suit your own specifications at a framer's or craft shop; you can renovate old frames bought from junk shops and market stalls; you can use frame kits or clip frames; or you can buy cheap framed prints, replacing the print with your mounted drawing. You can also order frames by post. Where possible, send for samples and details to check the quality and suitability before placing an order.

The choice of the frame moulding should obviously relate to the size and type of drawing, as well as the mount. Small drawings often look best with a plain, narrow moulding in natural wood, while larger works can take something proportionately wider. You might decide to use a plain coloured moulding for an abstract, whereas a detailed still life might look better in a more ornate frame. To help with ideas about framing, have a look around some galleries and exhibitions to see how other artists have framed their drawings.

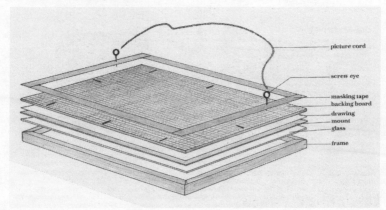

Illustration 12.3 Assembling the mount and drawing in the frame.

Making frames

Perhaps you are interested in making your own frames. If so, as well as enjoying the satisfaction that comes from having created both picture and frame, you will be able to ensure that the frame is made exactly to the specification you require for the drawing.

For framing, in addition to some basic woodworking equipment, you will need a good quality mitre saw, a frame clamp, an underpinner, a brad gun and a glasscutter. These can be purchased from some art and craft shops, hardware shops or through specialist suppliers. Additionally, you may find that some framing courses are available locally in the form of evening or day classes run by an adult education centre. Other courses are advertised in art magazines and directories.

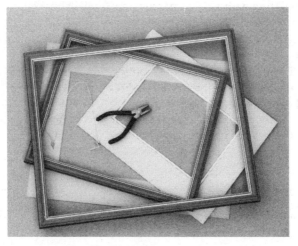

Illustration 12.4 Frames, mounts and framing accessories.

Displaying drawings

It is satisfying to see some of your drawings displayed around the house. Where and how they are hung is, of course, a matter for your own judgement, but there are one or two points to bear in mind when considering the siting of pictures.

Avoid placing a framed drawing in a position where it will get a lot of full sunlight, as eventually exposure of this sort will cause fading and discolouration, both to the mount and the drawing. In fact, the position of a picture with regard to the source of light, whether natural or artificial, is important. If it is placed so that the picture glass reflects various other items or parts of the room, the drawing will be difficult to view. As a rough guide, where possible, hang pictures so that the centre of the drawing is slightly below your eye level. Drawings often look better if arranged and displayed in groups rather than in isolation, particularly if they are small.

Insight

You can add variety to your display by changing the drawings in the fames or by moving the framed drawings around to different rooms.

The other point to watch out for is humidity and dampness. A framed drawing placed against a cold stone wall, for example, will gradually pull out any dampness from the wall, or alternatively, trap condensation. Check the backs of frames occasionally to see if there are any signs of dampness.

10 THINGS TO REMEMBER

1 *Framing some of your drawings will give you a lot of pleasure and will spur you on to produce even better work in the future.*

2 *You could display your framed drawings in your own home or even enter them for exhibitions.*

3 *Before framing a drawing, check it over to see if there are any final details or alterations you need to make.*

4 *Depending on the type of drawing, it may need fixing (spraying with fixative) and backing before choosing the mount and frame.*

5 *Aim for mounts and frames that are not too dominant yet will present your drawing to the best effect.*

6 *Mounts should be cut with a slightly wider margin at the bottom than at the sides and top.*

7 *Double mounts often give a more pleasing professional look.*

8 *It is important that mounts and fames are well made, or they will detract rather than enhance your work.*

9 *If you are not confident about making your own mounts and frames, take your drawing to a professional framer.*

10 *Never hang framed drawings where there is any possibility of dampness or, contrastingly, full sunlight.*

Glossary of drawing terms

aerial perspective The influence of the atmosphere on a distant view so that objects are less distinct, tonal contrasts muted, and colours weaker and cooler. Colours often seem to acquire a bluish tinge as they recede.

airbrush A mechanical tool for creating finely controlled spray effects. Compressed air from a canister or compressor is mixed with the paint and directed through an adjustable nozzle to make the spray.

asymmetrical A design or shape which, when divided along its central axis (more or less in half), is not identically balanced.

bleed The blurring of the edges of a line or shaded area caused when two wet areas meet, a wet wash undercuts a dry charcoal or pastel area, or a wet medium is applied over a dry one. This can also happen when ink or brush lines are applied to certain types of paper.

blending The fading of one colour into another or the working together of adjacent areas of shading or tone to create a gradual transition from light to dark. Blending works best with a soft drawing medium such as charcoal, pastel or a 6B pencil. You can blend colours or tones by rubbing them together with your fingers, a rag or a paper torchon.

blocking in Establishing the main areas of tone or colour in a drawing, usually in a fairly quick, loose manner. The process is most relevant to larger, more expressive drawings in charcoal, pastel and conté. The blocked-in areas serve as a sort of underdrawing that is subsequently modified and developed with the necessary detail.

burnishing A technique sometimes used in pencil drawings, particularly coloured pencil drawings, in which the tones or colours are rubbed into each other and worked into the paper surface using a torchon. As a result, the coloured pigments and graphite tones are compressed, intensified, and take on a slight sheen.

centre of vision The point on the horizon or at eye level which is immediately in front of you. This need not be in the middle of the drawing because your viewpoint could be from one side.

chiaroscuro Dramatic contrasts of light and dark as, for example, in the drawings of Leonardo da Vinci and Rembrandt.

cockling (buckling) Uneven paper surface after applications of wash or spray.

composition The way you arrange the various shapes and content of your drawing into a particular design.

contour drawing Concentrating on the outlines of the different shapes yet at the same time aiming to convey three-dimensional form.

draughtsmanship Skill in drawing.

drawing process All the stages involved in making a drawing, from the initial idea and thumbnail sketches through to the completed drawing.

elements of drawing Line, point, tone, texture, colour, form, size, shape and pattern.

eye level An actual or imagined horizontal line in a drawing which represents your line of vision in relation to the subject and shows the position from which your viewpoint is taken.

figurative The same as representational: a drawing of something real rather than imagined or abstract.

figure drawing A drawing of a human figure.

fixative A kind of very thin varnish which is sprayed over soft pencil, charcoal and pastel drawings to prevent them smudging.

focal point The object or part of the drawing that most attracts your attention. Usually the design or composition is so devised that shapes and lines lead your eye to a particular point.

foreshortening The influence of perspective on an object coming directly towards you, such as an outstretched arm. This gives a very obvious contrast in scale between the nearest part and that furthest away.

form The three-dimensional shape of something.

foxing Brown spots on a drawing caused by exposure to dampness.

Golden Section The use of a mathematical proportion known since Classical times and believed to possess exceptional aesthetic qualities. The ratio is approximately 5:8, although artists tend to approximate this further in terms of thirds. Therefore in a composition, the main feature, or focal point, is often placed about one third of the way across the picture area.

gradation The gradual transition from light to dark shading without any noticeable edges.

grid Division of the drawing into squares to help with the organization of the composition and scale, or for enlarging.

hatching Short, closely spaced straight lines used to suggest shadows or texture. The lines are usually slanting and the closer they are together, the more intense is the shading effect. In cross-hatching, a series of lines drawn in one direction is overworked with others in the opposite direction.

highlight The very lightest area in a drawing. A part that attracts or reflects the greatest amount of light.

horizon line A horizontal line, drawn or imagined, which represents your eye level and the furthest point of sight on the ground area.

image An object or figure. The general shape and likeness of something.

landscape As well as drawings of the open countryside, this relates to the general shape of a drawing in which the horizontal measurement is significantly greater than the vertical one.

lifting out In charcoal or soft pencil drawings, highlights and details can be removed or lifted out from dark shaded areas using a putty eraser or pencil eraser.

light-box A device used for making tracings. It consists of a box with a clear Perspex lid, lit from inside.

masking fluid A rubber compound solution that is painted on to particular areas to protect them from general wash or spray applications. You can use it to 'save' highlights, fine lines and small details. It can be applied at any stage in a drawing, either to preserve patches of white paper or a particular colour or effect. When the drawing is finished, the masking fluid can be rubbed off or picked away.

medium Any drawing material, such as pencil, charcoal, pastel, and ink.

mixed media Using several different drawing tools or materials within the same drawing.

modelling Creating the impression of three-dimensional form by using contrasts of light and dark.

monochrome A drawing in black and white or confined to a range of tones of one colour.

monotone Using a single tone (shade) plus areas of white; normally black and white.

natural forms Shells, bark, plants and other objects found in nature.

objective drawing A drawing in which the intention is to be as accurate as possible and to show a real likeness of something.

overworking Adding more work, perhaps in a different medium or technique, over parts of the drawing already completed.

perspective A technique for creating the illusion of distance and space.

portrait A drawing of someone's head and shoulders. This term is also used to describe the shape of a drawing in which the vertical dimension is greater than the horizontal one.

proportion The size of one object in relation to others. Also, the size of one part of an object in relation to other parts and to the object as a whole.

register Keeping one sheet of paper exactly in the right position in relation to a sheet beneath, when making monoprints, tracings and copies.

representational drawing A drawing which shows something exactly as you see it.

rough A quick preliminary sketch to try out an idea.

sgraffito Drawings made by scratching through one layer of colour or tone to reveal a contrasting one beneath. For example, you can scratch lines into black ink which has been applied over coloured wax crayon.

shading Creating light and dark areas in a drawing to give the effect of shadows and the illusion of three-dimensional form.

silverpoint A technique for making delicate line drawings using a silver-pointed instrument on paper coated with a slightly abrasive ground of white pigment.

stippling Creating tone or mixed colour by holding a brush, pencil or pen vertically and stabbing it up and down to produce an area of fine dots.

stretching paper Preparing paper by taping it to a board, so any subsequent washes of ink or paint do not distort its surface.

support Anything used to draw on, like paper and card.

symmetrical A completely balanced composition or shape. If divided in half, one half would be a mirror image of the other.

technique The process of working in a particular drawing medium or the individual method of using that medium, such as hatching, stippling or linear.

template A shape cut from thin card which can be used to draw round in order to repeat the outline several times.

thumbnail sketch A very small sketch just to show the simple outlines of an idea.

tint Weak colour. Usually a thin colour wash added to a drawing.

tone The relative lightness or darkness of a colour or the progression from black through various greys to white.

tooth The grain or surface texture of paper. This is particularly relevant to charcoal and pastel drawings, which rely on a rough or textured surface to hold the medium in place.

torchon (or Tortillon) A rolled paper stump, rather like a small pencil, that is used for blending and burnishing techniques.

vanishing point Lines used in perspective will appear to converge to a point on the horizon or eye level, known as the vanishing point.

wash Ink or paint diluted to a very fluid state and lightly applied over the paper surface.

Taking it further

Instructional magazines

The Artist	www.painters-online.co.uk
Artists and Illustrators	www.artistsandillustrators.co.uk
The Artist's Magazine	www.artistsnetwork.com/artistsmagazine
The International Artist	www.international-artist.com
Leisure Painter	www.painters-online.co.uk

Publishers of books on drawing

Batsford	www.anovabooks.com
David & Charles	www.davidandcharles.co.uk
Dorling Kindersley	www.dk.com
Dover Publications	http://store.doverpublications.com
North Light Books	www.fwbookstore.com/category/north-light
Phaidon Press	www.phaidon.com
Search Press	www.searchpress.com
Sterling Publishing Co. Inc.	www.sterlingpub.com
Thames & Hudson	www.thamesandhudson.com
Watson-Guptill	www.watson-guptill.com

Demonstration DVDs

APV Films	www.apvfilms.com
Teaching Art Ltd	www.teachingart.co.uk
Town House Films	www.townhousefilms.co.uk

Courses

Adult Residential Colleges Association	www.arca.uk.net
Artcourses.co.uk	www.artcourses.co.uk
Cheltenham Tutorial College	www.cheltenhamlearning.co.uk
The London Art College	www.londonartcollege.co.uk
The Open College of the Arts	www.oca-uk.com
Painting Holiday Directory	www.paintingholidaydirectory.com

Drawing materials suppliers

Artifolk	www.artifolk.co.uk
Great Art	www.greatart.co.uk
Heaton Cooper Studio	www.heatoncooper.co.uk
Jackson's Art Supplies	www.jacksonsart.co.uk
Ken Bromley Art Supplies	www.artsupplies.co.uk
L. Cornelissen & Son	www.cornelissen.com
Millers Art	www.millers-art.com
Paintworks	www.paintworks.biz
The Art Materials Company	www.artmaterialsco.com
T. N. Lawrence	www.lawrence.co.uk

Index

Illustrations not contained by the text page range are indicated in roman. Plates are indicated by the prefix pl.